WHEN CORPORATIONS LEAVE

WHEN CORPORATIONS LEAVE TOWN

*The Costs and Benefits
of Metropolitan Job Sprawl*

JOSEPH PERSKY
WIM WIEWEL

Wayne State University Press
Detroit

Manufactured in the United States of America

04 03 02 01 00   5 4 3 2 1

Library of Congress Cataloging-in-Publication Data

Persky, Joseph.
    When corporations leave town : the costs and benefits of metropolitan job sprawl / Joseph Persky, Wim Wiewel.
       p.   cm.
    Includes bibliographical references and index.
    ISBN 0-8143-2907-1   (alk. paper) — ISBN 0-8143-2908-x   (pbk. : alk. paper)
       1. Industrial location—Illinois—Chicago Metropolitan Area—Decision making—Mathematical models.   2. Land use, Urban—Environmental aspects—Illinois—Chicago Metropolitan Area—Costs—Mathematical models.   3. Land use, Rural—Environmental aspects—Illinois—Chicago Metropolitan Area—Costs—Mathematical models.   4. Deindustrialization—Illinois—Chicago Metropolitan Area—Costs—Mathematical models.   5. Urbanization—Illinois—Chicago Metropolitan Area—Costs—Mathematical models.   6. Plant shutdowns—Illinois—Chicago Metropolitan Area—Sociological aspects—Mathematical models.   7. Finance, Local—Illinois—Chicago Metropolitan Area—Mathematical models.   I. Wiewel, Wim.   II. Title.
HC108.C4 P47 2000
338.6'042'0977311—dc21

                                                                  000-009540

CONTENTS

List of Tables and Figures   7

Acknowledgments   9

CHAPTER 1   **Metropolitan Deconcentration**   11

    1.1 What is Deconcentration?   12
    1.2 Central City Development and Deconcentration   15
    1.3 Deconcentration and Outer Suburbs   18
    1.4 Deconcentration and Inner Suburbs   20
    1.5 From Rhetoric to Measurement   22

CHAPTER 2   **Is Manufacturing Deconcentration**
             Efficient?   23

    2.1 The Setting   25
    2.2 Manufacturing Jobs and People   27
    2.3 Externalities   34
    2.4 Public-Sector Costs   51
    2.5 Private Benefits and Costs   64
    2.6 Summing Up   71

CHAPTER 3   **Distributional Consequences**   73

    3.1 The Distribution of Externalities   73
    3.2 The Distribution of Public Subsidy Costs   80
    3.3 The Distribution of Private Benefits   83
    3.4 The Overall Distribution of Gains and Losses   86

CHAPTER 4   **Business Services Deconcentration**   89

    4.1 Jobs and People   89
    4.2 Externalities   91
    4.3 Public-Sector Costs   93

4.4 Private Benefits   93
4.5 Total Costs and Benefits   94
4.6 Distribution of Costs and Benefits   95

CHAPTER 5   **Dealing With Metropolitan
             Deconcentration**   99

5.1 Policies That Constrain Deconcentration or Better
    Allocate Costs   101
5.2 Policies That Redistribute the Benefits of Growth   113
5.3 Policies That Enhance Competitiveness   124
5.4 Conclusions   130

APPENDIX A1 **Calculations**   135

A1.1 Site, Residence, Household Income, and Gender   135
A1.2 The Multiplier   136
A1.3 Externalities   138
A1.4 Public-Sector Impacts   141
A1.5 Private Benefits and Costs, Resident Benefits
     and Costs   145
A1.6 Distribution   149

APPENDIX A2 **The Inner Suburbs**   152

A2.1 Inner Suburbs and Manufacturing Externalities   153
A2.2 Inner Suburbs and Business Services   156

APPENDIX A3 **Basic Theory**   159

Notes   163

Bibliography   169

Index   179

TABLES AND FIGURES

TABLES

1-1. Declining and Growing Central Cities: Sixteen Largest Metropolitan Areas   13

1-2. Population and Land Growth of Metropolitan Areas   14

1-3. Outer Suburban Growth of Population and Employment   19

2-1. Automobile Commuting Statistics for Workers Employed at City and Suburban Workplaces, Chicago Metropolitan Area, 1990   36

2-2. Effective Auto Time per Worker for Fifty-Four Worker Types, Chicago Metropolitan Area, 1990   37

2-3. Estimates of Marginal Social Costs of Peak-Hour Traffic   38

2-4. Estimates of Annual Accident Costs Imposed on Others   40

2-5. Estimates of Automobile Pollution Costs Imposed on Others   40

2-6. Annual Externalities Generated by New Electrical Equipment Plant   50

2-7. Costs Imposed by a New City Household as Share of Average City Costs per Household   56

2-8. Annual Net Local Fiscal Impact per New Household by Income Group and Location   57

2-9. Annual Increase in Public-Sector Costs Associated with the Choice of a Greenfield Location Rather Than a Chicago Location   63

2-10. Annual Private Benefits and Costs of Employment Decentralization   72

2-11. Annual Costs and Benefits of Choosing Greenfield Development   72

3-1. Distribution of Externalities by Household Income   79

3-2. Distribution of Externalities by Place of Residence   80

3-3. Distribution of Public-Sector Costs by Household Income   83

3-4. Distribution of Public-Sector Costs by Geography 83

3-5. Distribution of Private Benefits by Household Income 86

3-6. Distribution of Private Benefits by Geography 86

3-7. Overall Distribution of Costs and Benefits by Household Income Groups 87

3-8. Overall Distribution of Costs and Benefits by Residential Location 87

4-1. Annual Externalities Generated by New Business Services Facility Locating in the Outer Suburbs Rather Than Central City 92

4-2. Annual Public-Sector Costs from Business Services Facility Locating in the Outer Suburbs Rather Than Central City 93

4-3. Annual Private Benefits of Employment Decentralization 93

4-4. Annual Total Benefits and Costs of Deconcentration of Business Service Employment 94

4-5. Overall Distribution of Costs and Benefits by Household Income Groups 96

4-6. Overall Distribution of Costs and Benefits by Residential Location 96

5-1. Summary Comparison of Policies 131

A1-1. Determinants of Wages for Men and Women in Metropolitan Chicago 148

A2-1. Costs and Benefits of Inner Suburban Devleopment of an Electrical Equipment Plant 155

A2-2. Costs and Benefits of Inner Suburban Devleopment of a Business Services Facility 158

FIGURES

2-1. Where Manufacturing Workers Live 28

2-2. Manufacturing Workers by Household Income 29

3-1. Distribution of Congestion Externality Across Income Groups 75

3-2. Distribution of Population and Income Across Income Groups 76

3-3. Income Shares of Each Income Group by Residence 81

4-1. Residential Distribution of Service Workers by Facility Site 90

4-2. Distribution of Service Workers Across Income Groups 91

ACKNOWLEDGMENTS

We thank Mark Sendzik who made major contributions as a research assistant. In addition, we drew on the talents of Dan McGrath, Jessica Rio, and Kim Schaffer. We also thank the Lincoln Institute of Land Policy, which provided a generous grant for us to finish this project as well as the MacArthur Foundation, which supported the initial research as part of the City of Chicago's Brownfield Forum. We owe a considerable debt of gratitude to Janice Weiss, who undertook to render intelligible our less than peerless prose. Whatever awkwardness remains is certainly not her fault. We also thank the reviewers and Arthur Evans of Wayne State University Press, David Merriman of Loyola University, and Robert Bruegmann at the University of Illinois at Chicago for their insightful comments. Finally, the Great Cities Institute of the College of Urban Planning and Public Affairs at the University of Illinois at Chicago provided a most hospitable environment for our work. Earlier versions of some of this work have previously appeared in two journals—*Infrastructure* and *Policy Studies Journal*—and in chapters from two books—*The End of Welfare* (Max Sawicky, editor, M. E. Sharpe) and *Urban-Suburban Interdependencies* (Rosalind Greenstein and Wim Wiewel, editors, Lincoln Institute of Land Policy).

CHAPTER 1

Metropolitan Deconcentration

For more than a quarter of a century, some of the largest cities in the northeastern and midwestern United States have been losing employment. Industrial plants have been left to decay, while neighborhood commercial strips have fallen into abandonment. At the same time, in the outer suburbs of these cities, large corporations have erected new facilities on former farmland, and supermalls have risen on greenfield sites. This book presents our assessment of the costs and benefits of these trends.

Mainstream American attitudes toward cities and suburbs are intensely contradictory. On the one hand, the collective American dream paints the orderly tree-lined suburb as embodying our traditional values of privacy and community. Low-density suburban living beckons as the pleasurable reward for personal effort. Work, too, seems safer and more pleasant in a suburban setting, whether in a new factory or office complex. In sum, suburban life seems to be what Americans work for, what Americans want, and what Americans envision as good.

Despite the strength of such images, the American "big city" still has its allure, with its siren song of sparkling office towers, medical complexes, cultural events, social diversity, and bustling crowds. This cultural schizophrenia has helped fuel the debate about metropolitan deconcentration. Drawing on widespread stereotypes of city and suburb, some scholars have simply picked sides and come out slugging.

Disagreements about the appropriate role of planning in a market economy have only added to the heat. Some have argued that suburbanization is the result of free choice in a free economy: Americans simply prefer the low-density living arrangements, and firms make higher profits, in the suburbs. Exponents of this perspective often argue that metropolitan planning does not advance the common interest, but only champions the narrow aspirations of an unrepresentative collection of cultural elitists and city property owners. Leave the market alone, they argue, and efficiency will result.

Many city planners and critics of suburban sprawl have strongly contested this benevolent portrayal of market forces. In their view, pollution, congestion, and the destruction of open space have proliferated because they have been left unpriced in the market. Government at all levels has tolerated privately created spillover costs or externalities; in fact, government has promoted metropolitan sprawl through its transportation and tax policies. Rather than regulating market forces, the public sector has compromised its responsibilities and subsidized the growth machine.

In the midst of these broad cultural and ideological debates, the meaning of city job losses is easily obscured by rhetorical excess on all sides. To bring some light to this heated argument, this book presents our systematic reckoning of the costs and benefits of employment deconcentration. We consider a wide range of effects, their net impact, and their distribution. We focus on the most striking cases—metropolitan areas whose central cities are experiencing absolute declines or deconcentration of employment. In addition to assessing the impact of deconcentration, we also examine a range of public interventions intended to reverse, slow, or meliorate the trend. Throughout, we strive to be evenhanded and balanced.

1.1 WHAT IS DECONCENTRATION?

From a spatial perspective, a metropolitan area's population and employment can grow in only two ways—by spreading development at the outside margins, or by increasing density within already built-up areas. This is the simple logic of land use. But regardless of where they locate, new households and firms face rising costs. At the periphery, higher costs take the form of reduced access to the rest of the metropolitan area. At the center, higher costs are due to increased congestion and the higher rents that result from increased demand.

In general, one might expect growth to occur both in the center and at the margins of a metropolitan area. Indeed, this is the case in the newer, more rapidly growing metropolitan areas of the Southwest and West. However, over the past twenty-five years, many of the older cities of the Northeast and Midwest have experienced real declines in their central city populations, while their suburban populations have been rising. This is the phenomenon we call population deconcentration (see table 1-1). It has occurred primarily in older cities that had relatively high population densities in their central cities—an average of more than 14,200 people per square mile in 1970, compared with 5,160 in other, newer large cities. Many of the shrinking cities have experienced

TABLE 1-1.

Declining and Growing Central Cities: Sixteen Largest
Metropolitan Areas

Cities	Population Change, 1970–1990 (city only) %	Employment Change, 1970–1990 (city only) %	Population Density, 1970 (city only) thousands of persons/sq. mile
Declining Population			
New York	−7.2	5.5	26.3
Chicago	−17.3	−8.0	15.1
Philadelphia	−18.6	−14.3	15.1
Detroit	−32.0	−38.3	11.0
Boston	−10.4	12.3	13.9
Washington	−19.8	27.4	12.4
Cleveland	−32.6	−24.8	9.9
St. Louis	−36.2	−15.1	10.2
Average	−22.6	−6.9	14.2
Growing Population			
Los Angeles	23.8	48.6	6.1
San Francisco–Oakland	1.7	21.9	11.0
Houston	32.4	91.6	3.1
Dallas–Fort Worth	17.5	59.5	2.6
Miami	7.2	62.6	9.8
San Diego	59.9	109.7	3.3
San Jose	76.1	147.2	3.8
Phoenix	156.8	132.0	1.5
Average	46.9	84.1	5.2

Source: U. S. Census, 1970 and 1990.

Note: The first group above includes the eight largest urbanized areas in 1970 with central cities experiencing population declines between 1970 and 1990. The second group includes the eight largest urbanized areas in 1970 with central cities experiencing population growth between 1970 and 1990.

employment deconcentration as well as population declines. These losses are particularly striking since the period under consideration, 1970–90, witnessed much faster employment growth than population growth.

Deconcentration is not simply a matter of physical expansion. All of the metropolitan areas we studied have grown in land area (see table 1-2). But in newer metropolises of the West and Southwest, physical expansion has lagged behind population growth (Los Angeles, Dallas–Fort Worth, San Diego, and Phoenix). For example, in Phoenix, land area increased by 90% between 1970 and 1990, but population increased by 130%. By contrast, in Washington, D.C., land area increased by

TABLE 1-2.

Population and Land Area Growth of Metropolitan Areas

Metropolitan Area	Population Change, urbanized area 1970–1990 (%)	Land Area Change, urbanized area 1970–1990 (%)	Population Density, 1970 (thousands of persons/sq. mi.)	Population Density, 1990 (thousands of persons/sq. mi.)
Declining Central City Population				
New York	−1.0	22.3	6.7	5.4
Chicago	1.2	24.0	5.3	4.3
Philadelphia	5.0	54.8	5.4	3.6
Detroit	−6.9	28.3	4.5	3.3
Boston	4.6	34.2	4.0	3.1
Washington, D.C.	35.6	91.3	5.0	3.6
Cleveland	−14.4	−1.6	3.0	2.6
St. Louis	3.4	57.9	4.1	2.7
Average	3.4	38.9	4.7	3.6
Growing Central City Population				
Los Angeles	36.6	25.1	5.3	5.8
San Francisco– Oakland	21.5	28.3	4.4	4.2
Houston	72.9	183.7	4.1	2.5
Dallas–Fort Worth	58.6	34.9	1.9	2.2
Miami	57.0	36.3	4.7	5.4
San Diego	96.0	81.1	3.1	3.4
San Jose	40.0	22.0	3.7	4.3
Phoenix	132.4	91.0	2.2	2.7
Average	64.4	62.8	3.7	3.8

Source: U. S. Census, 1970 and 1990.

over 90%, population by only 36%. In both Philadelphia and St. Louis, land area increased by about 50%, while populations remained virtually constant.

While metropolitan areas throughout the country are physically expanding at a dramatic rate, it is primarily in the older, high-density metropolitan areas that densities are actually falling. Because of deconcentration, density in these areas has declined to levels more similar to those of the newer areas of the West and Southwest. Indeed, there has been a marked convergence in densities nationwide, as table 1-2 reveals. In 1970 the deconcentrating areas had metropolitan area population densities averaging 4,700 people per square mile as compared to 3,700 for the growing areas. In 1990, the average metropolitan population density among deconcentrating urban areas was actually lower than that of the newer urban areas—3,600 people per square mile versus 3,800.

Deconcentrating metropolitan areas are also characterized by relatively slower overall growth rates. Rapid metropolitan growth generates considerable investment in central city residential structures and commercial activities. These investments, linked to urban services and amenities, respond to the areawide expansion. They provide a more than adequate offset to any declines in manufacturing. Cities in this situation are not likely to deconcentrate. But in slow-growth metropolitan areas, demand for central city-based activities necessarily increases at a much more modest rate. It is true that the nationwide expansion of producer services and a renewed interest in urban living stimulate downtown. But without the stimulus of strong, metropolitan-wide growth, the expansion in these more centralized activities fails to outpace continuing losses in manufacturing and other activities drifting away from the center.

1.2 CENTRAL CITY DEVELOPMENT AND DECONCENTRATION

Older central cities have become increasingly heterogeneous over time. Fueled by the expansion of the information-service economy and its highly educated workforce, industrial cities such as Pittsburgh and Cleveland have enjoyed something of a renaissance as their downtowns have become stable magnets of high consumption, entertainment, and culture. But in the shadow of new downtown office towers, these cities have also suffered massive declines in manufacturing employment and increases in poverty. While high-visibility renovations and gentrification proceed, more and more neighborhoods have become part of the ghettos of the poor.

The rapid growth of business services and other office-based activities in the 1980s stimulated an office building boom throughout the country. Much of this boom occurred in the emerging outer suburbs, to which many corporate headquarters and sections of banks and insurance companies opted to relocate. But the central business districts of many older metropolitan areas also enjoyed a strong recovery, for numerous large law firms, specialized accountants, and advertising agencies chose to remain "downtown," where formal and informal information flowed freely and face-to-face contact was easy.[1]

Today, the downtowns of older cities do not dominate their metropolitan regions as they once did in the twentieth century, but they have escaped the dire fate that many predicted for them in the 1970s. Downtowns have not disappeared, and few metropolitan regions are doughnuts. While edge cities compete with older central business districts for the expanding service and information industries, the central business districts retain their focal roles in their regions' economic geography.

Part of the reason for the "rebirth" of these older cities lies with the younger generation of skilled workers and professionals connected to the information-service economy. They have gentrified architecturally interesting city neighborhoods, created a vast market for restaurants of all types, and sought entertainment and culture in the city. Even if many have ultimately moved out to the suburbs, their extended city residencies have infused a large amount of purchasing power into city economies. Older cities have also benefited from empty-nesters and retired people looking for stimulating environments. Among other services, this demographic group has also provided much of the demand that gave rise to mushrooming urban medical centers.

But the thriving central business district and adjacent affluent residential areas hardly comprise the entire city. In fact, the majority of the city's population has experienced wrenching structural change. Large numbers of manufacturing jobs have left the city, as have large numbers of middle-class residents. The number of city jobs still far exceeds the number of city residents. But an ever-increasing proportion of city jobs—between one-fourth and one-half—is held by suburban commuters, and the latter take home 40% to 65% of all central city earnings (Persky, Sclar, and Wiewel, 1992). Skill requirements have changed rapidly as the city has become increasingly specialized in high-end professional and business services (Kasarda, 1990). For low-skilled central city residents, there are few jobs in either the neighborhoods or downtown, and they cannot easily commute or move to the suburbs. Thus, for these people, the distributional consequences of metropolitan growth patterns have been disastrous.

As working-class and lower-middle-class families have continued to move out to the suburbs, older cities have become more unequal—the home of both the affluent and the poor. On the one hand, more prosperous areas have added restaurants and services. But in the rest of the city, neighborhood economies have declined as retail activities have contracted and few other sources of employment have emerged. Even when money comes into these depressed neighborhoods, it leaves almost instantaneously. A recent study of Buffalo suggests that every dollar of income earned in the depressed quadrant of the city stimulates only $0.06 of additional economic activity in the area (Cole, 1994).

In addition to such distributional consequences, deconcentration also has an impact on efficiency. Suburban sprawl in general creates spillover costs and public fiscal costs, but these are magnified by deconcentration. For example, when a metropolitan area is growing, the very poor may go homeless, but housing is in strong demand. But in a deconcentrating metropolitan area, as population declines, there is little to halt neighborhood deterioration and housing abandonment.

Deconcentration has even greater effects on public finance. Central cities are almost always poorer than their distant suburbs. But in deconcentrating metropolitan areas, this problem is exacerbated by the burden of maintaining a substantial stock of fixed capital. In the face of population declines, a deconcentrating city must still support and maintain its considerable infrastructures. At best a shrinking population is followed by only modest declines in these maintenance costs. For a range of public services, these deconcentrating cities are left with excess physical capacity. Where emerging suburban communities of the periphery must add new infrastructure to match their population growth, cities that have experienced population declines in the recent past can absorb considerable population growth without such expensive capital projects.

Deconcentration, with its implied waste of existing public and private resources, may seriously magnify the spillover costs of sprawl. To the extent that central city development could reduce urban poverty and anchor middle-income neighborhoods, such development would produce substantial savings for the entire metropolitan area.

Yet at the same time, countervailing forces may also exist. It is true that deconcentrating cities are likely to generate substantial spillovers of sprawl. But because these cities have high population density, many of their residents may place a high value on reducing the population density where they live. Thus the private gains associated with low-density, outer suburban lifestyles may be greater here than elsewhere. Under these circumstances, the spread of employment to the outer suburbs may allow city dwellers to reap large private gains by changing their places of residence and employment.

Employment deconcentration also promises gains to current suburban residents who commute into the city for work. These individuals place a high value on their suburban lifestyle—perhaps high enough to justify the cost of commuting to their jobs. If they can find employment more easily in the suburbs, their real welfare increases.

These same gains suggest that in deconcentrating areas, the profitability of outer suburban business locations will be relatively greater. This conclusion follows in part from the willingness of outer suburban workers to share some of their welfare gains with outer suburban employers, who offer relatively convenient employment opportunities with low commuting costs. Private gains such as these are real and must be included in any quantitative study of the effects of deconcentration.

This quick review of conditions in deconcentrating cities makes a key point. These cities and their metropolitan areas offer us the sharpest contrasts. Very likely, population and employment sprawl in these areas produce greater benefits *and* greater costs than in the new, more homogeneous metropolitan areas of the West and Southwest. The benefits are greater because the high-density cities of deconcentrating areas contrast sharply with their low-density outer suburbs. In the new metropolitan areas the difference between city and outer suburbs is much more modest. On the other hand, the costs of outer suburban growth are higher in deconcentrating areas because growth there leaves behind underfinanced public infrastructure and hard-strapped poverty populations in the cities.

1.3 DECONCENTRATION AND OUTER SUBURBS

Outer suburbs of deconcentrating metropolitan areas are growing. It is difficult to measure this growth, since it is not always easy to differentiate between outer and inner suburbs. However, three such areas—Chicago, Cleveland, and Detroit—illustrate the trend and also have relatively simple suburban geographies. Like other deconcentrating metropolitan areas, these three did not grow appreciably over the period; indeed, in Cleveland and Detroit, metropolitan population actually fell. Yet population in the outer suburbs of these cities grew by an average of 36%, and employment in the outer suburbs grew by an average of 109% (see table 1-3).

The employment growth of outer suburbs has been characterized by a highly decentralized sprawl, punctuated by the relatively dense concentration of so-called edge cities (Garreau, 1991). While outer suburban employment growth typically has started with light manufacturing and shopping malls, these have been followed by more white-collar service employment. New office buildings have risen in clusters and brought supporting activities such as restaurants, hotels, and business services (Stanback, 1991).

The vast majority of outer suburban jobs are held by people who live in those suburbs or in nearby inner suburbs. In part, this is because outer suburban worksites are hard to reach from the city. But in addition, outer suburban workers have a strong economic incentive to seek out housing in the less dense and cheaper lands even farther from the central city. This is economic common sense, reflecting the fact that land prices fall with distance from the center.

Housing developers bank on this fact; in their effort to provide an attractive product at low cost, they have a powerful incentive to build on greenfield sites. But the resulting housing developments necessarily require the expansion of local public services and infrastructure— new roads, sewers, and schools. While the housing may be cheap, this

TABLE 1-3.

Outer Suburban Growth of Population and Employment

Metropolitan Area	*Outer Suburban Share 1969 (%)*	*Outer Suburban Growth, 1969–1995 (%)*	*Outer Suburban Share of Metropolitan Growth, 1969–1995 (%)*
Chicago			
Population (number of persons)	22.3	64.6	157.3
Total full- and part-time employment	17.8	144.1	72.4
Cleveland-Lorain-Elyria, Ohio			
Population (number of persons)	28.9	18.7	METRO AREA (-)
Total, full- and part-time employment	20.6	65.5	82.0
Detroit			
Population (number of persons)	40.0	26.0	METRO AREA (-)
Total full- and part-time employment	33.6	116.5	151.7

Source: Bureau of Economic Analysis: Regional Economic Information System.
Note: All figures based on current definition of the corresponding PMSA.

expansion is not. Critics of sprawl often argue that such expenditures are wasteful. In addition, they argue that the rush toward the periphery destroys open space and encourages a relatively expensive low-density lifestyle (Ewing, 1997). Yet some research has suggested that it may actually be cheaper to provide services at low density than at high density (Ladd, 1992). This finding deserves further study, as it has important implications for the relative costs of new high- and low-density developments.

But given the reality of deconcentration, the central question is not which kind of new development is most efficient. Rather, since cities and inner suburbs contain underutilized existing facilities, the question is whether it makes more sense to build new facilities or to use existing ones more intensively.

Increasingly, the new residents of the outer suburbs have been required to pay impact fees to cover a portion of the infrastructure and other costs associated with their location decisions. Now an accepted tool in local planning, such impact fees are designed to capture only the costs that residential development imposes on local government. They do not address spillover costs (such as loss of open space) that have no direct effect on suburban government budgets, impacts elsewhere in the metropolitan area, or public costs borne at the state or national level.

This points up a recurring dilemma of outer suburban development. Typically, the most recent family to move to a greenfield area is the most eager to pull up the gangplank and limit or even forbid further development. There is logic behind this apparent irony. Drawn by the relatively low cost and low density of such areas, new greenfield residents fear development that will fundamentally alter the character and quality of their lives. Indeed, the very process of developing outer suburbs undermines the attractiveness of such locations to many of their current residents. When new plants spring up on the urban periphery, the higher density and congestion they bring reduce the amenity value of their formerly semirural environment. Deconcentration is not a simple matter of city versus outer suburbs, or poor versus rich; much of the cost of deconcentration falls on existing residents of the exurban periphery.

Nevertheless, many outer suburbanites support and profit from the rapid development of their communities, as it brings opportunities for capital gains and new employment. Not surprisingly, then, the question of whether to encourage or restrain development is often the central political issue on the metropolitan periphery.

1.4 DECONCENTRATION AND INNER SUBURBS

Many older metropolitan areas still boast one or more vintage inner suburbs, like the high-income neighborhoods of their central cities, with rich tradition and high housing values. But while the outer suburbs of deconcentrating metropolitan areas have grown and prospered, an increasing number of their inner suburbs have declined in the wake of the growth machine. Many of these inner suburbs are now approaching economic crisis.

Many inner suburbs sprang up quickly after World War II. They promised all the elements of the developing suburban lifestyle at a low price. Lot sizes may have been smaller than those of older suburbs, and the construction was less than first-class, but demand was high. These inner suburbs attracted millions of former city residents—production workers, office workers, and lower-level professionals. Often, inner suburbs also attracted manufacturers who saw the relatively cheap land as a good place to build new space-extensive plants. These plants supported the property tax base while providing jobs.

In the 1980s and 1990s, inner suburbs in slow-growing, deconcentrating areas found themselves in direct competition with newer outer suburbs. Burdened with an aging housing stock, the inner suburbs are losing that contest. Like most Americans, inner suburban residents are highly mobile. When they see attractive opportunities farther out from the central city, they are likely to opt to move there, little hindered by a feeling of community commitment.

In addition, as residents move into and out of metropolitan areas, the steady turnover of metropolitan households allows for considerable demographic shifts among suburbs. Lacking attachments to any particular municipality, new in-migrants with middle or high incomes are likely to gravitate to the outer suburbs, with their more modern housing stock and facilities.

These normal processes of residential succession push mightily on the inner suburbs of older cities. Just as the city's blue-collar bungalows and three-flats of the 1920s became the homes of less affluent residents, so the housing stock of the inner suburbs now filters down the income ladder. Just as the old neighborhood moved from solidly working class to a more marginal status, so too these inner suburbs are changing.

Census data show that 35% of all suburbs experienced declining real median income between 1979 and 1989 (Gurwitt, 1993). Between 1980 and 1990, the poverty population in metropolitan suburbs grew by 17%; in large metropolitan areas it grew by 30%[2] (Frey and Fielding, 1995, p. 61). Increasingly, poverty is not just a central city problem; suburbs now account for a substantial and increasing share of it.

This basic phenomenon has been documented in considerable geographic detail for three deconcentrating metropolitan areas—Chicago, Philadelphia, and Minneapolis (Orfield, 1997). In each of these areas, high levels of poverty, single-parent households, and crime have spilled across city boundaries to take root in inner suburbs. At the same time, many of these suburbs have experienced declining per capita real tax bases and shrinking employment opportunities. Not surprisingly, retailers have followed their customers farther out. Just as the shift of middle-income populations from city neighborhoods to inner suburbs worked havoc on neighborhood retail centers, so now the inner suburbs are seeing their own shuttered malls. In many of these suburbs, manufacturing employment is also in decline. In part, this simply reflects the broader national shift from a manufacturing to an information-service economy. But industry, like population, also follows a life cycle. New start-up plants see little reason to seek out locations in declining communities with high tax rates. While properties there may be cheap, up-to-date new facilities can be constructed on greenfields, near where their potential labor force has already moved.

The process of economic decline threatens the ability of many inner suburbs to provide critical public services. Indeed, the fiscal situation of these inner suburbs may be far worse than that of neighboring central cities. After all, even as central cities lost population and industry to the suburbs, they still maintained central business districts. With the rise of the office economy, downtowns grew and prospered, thus offsetting to a degree the loss of property taxes on manufacturing. For the most part, inner suburbs facing deconcentration have no such cushion to fall back on. Increasingly, they must raise their tax rates to guarantee minimum service levels. This is why the poorest suburbs generally have the highest tax rates but lower levels of services. In turn, this fiscal pressure helps fuel the outward flight of middle-income populations.

In any number of ways, declining inner suburbs of deconcentrating metropolitan areas have more in common with their central city's neighborhoods than they do with the rapidly growing communities of the outer suburbs. While more than half the electorate may live in suburbs, not all suburbs are alike. Inner city suburban residents share many of the same concerns as lower-middle-class city residents. Thus in considering the costs and benefits of employment deconcentration, we must not only compare central city and outer suburb; we must also consider the arguments for encouraging inner suburban economic development.

1.5 FROM RHETORIC TO MEASUREMENT

When reduced to its essentials, the case against employment deconcentration rests on two fundamental claims. First, deconcentration is inefficient. The various spillovers created by deconcentration cost more than the private gains that motivate it. Second, deconcentration is inequitable. Its costs fall disproportionately on low- and moderate-income households, while its benefits accrue largely to the affluent. Both of these arguments derive from the broader debate over suburban sprawl. However, in older metropolitan areas experiencing deconcentration, the stakes are particularly high.

Both of these fundamental claims are essentially empirical. Of course, empirical data are not enough to drive policy singlehandedly. For example, even if both of the above claims are found to be empirically true, one might still reasonably conclude that the total measured effects of deconcentration do not warrant major public intervention. Nonetheless, the first step in sorting out the debate must clearly be empirical measurement. In the next chapter, we begin a reassessment of these issues, building on the tools of applied welfare economics or cost-benefit analysis.

CHAPTER 2

Is Manufacturing Deconcentration Efficient?

Advocates of central city reconstruction have been particularly concerned to slow or reverse the flight of manufacturing jobs to the suburbs. Historically, many manufacturing jobs have required only modest levels of formal schooling, yet have paid solid wages. In the first half of the twentieth century, low-skilled urban workers who landed manufacturing jobs could hope to climb out of poverty. As manufacturing has moved to the suburbs, however, its jobs have become less and less accessible to the central city poor. For decades now, liberal social scientists, following the initial insights of John Kain, have argued that the resulting mismatch creates major social costs for society.

In response, defenders of suburban expansion have argued that manufacturing is best suited to the low-density economy of the distant suburbs. Modern plants are large and require spacious lots. The use of truck transportation, rather than the earlier dependence on rail, opens up the entire expanse of suburban greenfields. Moreover, the urban periphery contains a well-trained labor force on which these plants can draw. In the absence of any special ties to the central city, it is natural for plants to seek the cheaper land and cheaper labor of the metropolitan periphery. Advocates of a laissez-faire policy toward manufacturing decentralization conclude that any public attempts to impede the movement of manufacturing to the suburbs will prove inefficient and costly to society.

When a company chooses a greenfield site at the fringes of a metropolis, it does so because it expects the private gains to be higher at such a location than elsewhere. Higher profits signal the efficient use of private resources, an important consideration. But do the private benefits outweigh the social costs imposed by further greenfield development— costs such as traffic congestion and loss of open space?

These are empirical questions, not ideological ones. For several decades, the two sides in the sprawl debate have largely talked past each other.

In the heat of argument, it may seem that they hopelessly disagree on fundamental values. But this is hardly the case. With few exceptions, both sides espouse a broad interest in social welfare and a sincere concern for the nation's poor; each side maintains that *its* approach will best serve the common good.[1] The only way to sort out this impasse, we believe, is by assessing both the private benefits and the social costs of industrial decentralization.

Fortunately, a large body of research already exists that lays the groundwork for such an assessment. In what follows, we draw on three major streams in this research: first, the quantitative analysis of external costs such as traffic congestion; second, the study of the fiscal impacts of new industrial development on local, state, and federal governments; third, the investigation of differences in land and labor costs across the metropolitan area.

We do not present any deep new theoretical structure for this analysis.[2] What is novel about our approach is our insistence that these empirical traditions can be usefully and consistently integrated into the framework of microsimulation. We examine the consequences that follow when a large manufacturing plant chooses a greenfield site over the central city. What types of workers are likely to find employment at that site? Where will they live? How will they travel to work? In what kinds of housing will they live? What public services will they demand? Our simulation forecasts the answers to these and similar questions for both greenfield and central city sites.

Our basic source for these demographic and behavioral characteristics is the Public Use Microdata Sample (PUMS) of the U.S. Bureau of the Census. This source facilitates our estimation of wage levels, new car purchases, and converted acres generated by new employment; but it cannot tell us the economic costs or benefits associated with these changes. To address these aspects, we turn to the research mentioned above. What is the true cost of another automobile on the highway? What is the dollar value of the public subsidy to a new tract home, or of employing a low-skilled worker? We feed the best empirical answers to such questions into our simulation in order to estimate the costs and benefits of greenfield developments.

The chapters that follow contrast the consequences of new industrial facilities in greenfield locations to the effects of similar developments in the central city. We compare the world with new development in the outer suburban periphery to the world with the same development in the city itself. This comparison addresses the question: "What difference does it make if a new firm locates in the outer suburbs of a deconcentrating metropolitan area rather than in the area's central city?" Alternatively, the estimates presented below can be viewed as measuring the long-run net effects if an existing central city facility were to close and move to the suburbs. The two problems are essentially identical if in the long run the labor force of a suburbanizing plant takes on the demographics of other similar plants in the outer suburbs.

Finally, before we plunge into the empirical effort, we must acknowledge the marginalist perspective that characterizes our approach. Most critics of suburban sprawl frame their case more broadly. They juxtapose the present situation against a very different scenario—one in which industrial location patterns bear little relation to those we currently observe, vacant land in the central city has been built up, public transportation has been improved, and growth controls limit suburban expansion. By contrast, we focus on the marginal changes whose effects can be reasonably extrapolated from current data and current knowledge. This is not because we believe those broader visions are wrong, but simply because our marginalist methodology of microsimulations cannot address such possibilities. Thus we estimate the effects of only modest shifts in employment between alternative locations. It is possible that much larger changes in geographic patterns would produce interactions or economies of agglomeration of such magnitudes as to alter dramatically the results reported here. Similarly, the present exercise takes as given a broad range of constraints in the political and economic sphere inherited from the status quo. For all of these reasons, our methodology represents a conservative point of view.

2.1 THE SETTING

What difference will it make if a new manufacturing plant picks a greenfield location rather than a site in the central city? To answer this fundamental question, we analyze and compare the implications of placing a hypothetical new electrical equipment plant with one thousand workers in two alternative sites: in the outer suburban ring of the Chicago metropolitan area, and in the central city of Chicago. The approach is that of cost-benefit analysis. The analysis is national in scope. In principle, the accounting includes every gain or loss following on this location decision.

We chose an electrical equipment plant as typical of the growth sector of manufacturing. In recent years, the electrical equipment industry has been expanding in the metropolitan Chicago area, mostly in the more distant suburbs. However, the following is not meant as a case study of any particular firm; just the opposite. In most respects, the estimates generated for this electrical equipment plant should be representative of those for a broad range of modern, solid wage, light manufacturing enterprises. Similarly, but with less confidence, we suggest that our estimates for the Chicago area are applicable to large metropolitan areas experiencing deconcentration.

Like any new facility, the proposed electrical equipment plant creates both benefits and costs. As we will show in detail, our analysis leads us to conclude that greenfield manufacturing development doesn't pay. A greenfield plant does generate substantial benefits for the company, but it also creates social costs, in the form of externalities and public-sector losses. While the precision of our calculations should not be overstated, they strongly suggest that the social costs of manufacturing deconcentration are of the same magnitude as the private gains that drive such development.

Perhaps these results can please none of the most aggressive parties to the debate over greenfield plants. Our estimates temper the most startling claims of both sides. Many urban reformers have argued that continuing suburbanization of industry is grossly inefficient; they clearly would expect the externalities and public costs to far outweigh the private benefits of the greenfield location. But such reformers have focused on suburban gridlock without considering that if a company locates in the city, many of its jobs will inevitably be held by suburbanites. These reformers have emphasized the costs of new suburban infrastructure without acknowledging that accommodating central city growth also requires new money for key city services. Similarly, they have seen the public costs associated with the loss of open space, but have neglected the gains to corporate productivity.

On the other hand, many economists and business representatives have asserted that the market pressures that promote suburbanization of industry reflect large efficiency gains achievable only in outer suburban locations. These apologists have insisted that externalities and public costs amount to only minor considerations. It would appear they are wrong. At the margin those costs just about equal the private gains achieved by deconcentration.

Are greenfield plants efficient? On net, we find that the answer appears to be a closer call than either side has suggested. Perhaps this result explains why the debate over greenfield industrial development has remained both acrimonious and unresolved. It is precisely when large forces net out that conflicts remain most intense.

Although our estimates fall between the most strident claims of greenfield opponents and defenders, in no way do they imply that greenfield development is a matter of indifference. Rather, they call into question policies that allow or even encourage a considerable and highly dubious transfer of resources, with no clear resulting gains in efficiency. These results also underscore the need for new policies that focus more sharply on the distributional implications of alternative industrial development patterns.

This conclusion rests on the plausibility of our estimates of the costs and benefits of greenfield manufacturing development. This chapter addresses the most significant analytical and empirical issues raised in these estimates. Our overview will provide an introduction to the interdependencies of metropolitan land use while clarifying our overall approach. First, we discuss our estimates of the number, location, and commuting patterns of new workers and new households under each scenario. Then we will discuss the externalities and public costs associated with these alternative locations, making dollar estimates of their value. Finally, we add the private costs and benefits, which will complete the picture of all costs and benefits associated with the plant's location decision.

2.2 MANUFACTURING JOBS AND PEOPLE

The social costs and benefits generated by any new plant depend critically on the character of its workers—where they live, what incomes they earn, what kind of housing they buy, how they get to work, and whether they would be unemployed in the absence of the plant. The location of a plant has a strong impact on these factors.

Where Workers Live

Not surprisingly, workers employed in outer suburban plants tend to live in the outer suburbs. According to figures calculated from the Census Bureau's 1990 Public Use Microdata Sample (PUMS), about 77% of manufacturing workers in Chicago area outer suburbs live in the outer suburbs. Only 7% reverse commute from the central city. By contrast, a manufacturing plant in the central city draws almost two-thirds of its workforce from city residents (see figure 2-1).

While the difference between the residential patterns of greenfield and central city workers is substantial, simply putting plants in the central city will by no means deliver all the resulting jobs to central city residents. In fact, more than one-third of central city jobs are held by suburban residents. The high level of commuting from suburban residences to city jobs limits several of the gains that might otherwise be associated with locating plants in the central city. As much as some planners might like to force all new city jobholders to live in the city and take the bus to work, assuming such an outcome will lead one to exaggerate the gains associated with central city development. In projecting the likely

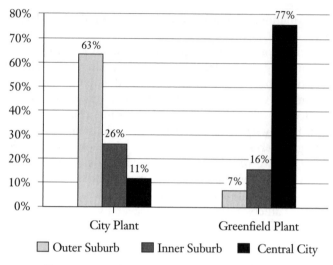

Figure 2-1. Where Manufacturing Workers Live

residential patterns of new workers, we take the current patterns of real workers as a guide.

Job Location and Household Income

Manufacturing workers in city plants are more likely to live in the city than workers in suburban sites. As a result, their commuting patterns and housing consumption will differ sharply from those of suburban workers. But these behaviors are also influenced by the overall income of a worker's household. To predict whether workers will commute by car or live in apartments, we must know something about their household incomes.

For any given occupation, workers in city plants tend to come from lower-income households than workers in similar suburban jobs. This is not because wages in the suburbs are higher; for workers with the same job skills, wages in the city actually tend to be higher or at least equal to those in the outer suburbs. Yet even if the city worker earns wages equal to those of the outer suburban worker, the former is likely to come from a household with lower overall income. This is especially true for low-skilled workers. In part, this is because low-skilled workers living in the city are more likely to be the primary or sole earner in their households. By contrast, low-skilled jobs in the outer suburbs are more likely to be held by a second or even third worker in a middle- or high-income household. For instance, a woman living in an outer suburb who takes an unskilled assembly job in a new greenfield plant may earn minimum wage, but will often come from a middle-income family. In the central city, the same job may provide the primary income for an entire household.

These observations are reflected in real differences in city and outer suburban labor forces. The PUMS makes it possible to link individuals to their households. Doing so reveals that manufacturing plants in the city of Chicago employ a higher proportion of individuals from low- and moderate-income households (25%) than do plants in the area's outer suburbs (17%; see figure 2-2).[3] In fact, city plants draw almost 50% more workers from low-income households than do greenfield plants. Among women, the difference is even larger. Again, this is because low-skilled workers in the outer suburbs are more likely to be secondary workers from middle- and high-income households.

We now have a rough picture of the residence and income level of the employees of existing manufacturing plants. If the employees of a new facility are likely to be similar, we can use these data to simulate the character and economic behavior of new workers and their households.

But is it reasonable for a simulation to assume that each new job brings with it a new household? The question is central, since several of our concerns relate to household and not individual behavior. For example, the purchase of a new dwelling in a greenfield tract (and hence the residential absorption of open space and an increase in outer suburban fiscal costs) is most often made by a household, not an individual. In general, we expect the number of new households to be less than the number of new workers. This is because many households have more

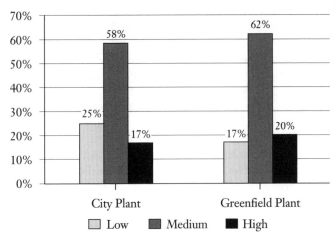

Figure 2-2. Manufacturing Workers by Household Income

than one wage earner. Each of these jobholders cannot individually be responsible for the location of his or her entire household, so the number of new households per worker will generally be less than one.

But simply dividing households by workers is still likely to yield an overestimate of the number of new households generated by the creation of new jobs. Many new entrants to the labor force adjust their job search to their residential location, not vice versa. For such workers, residential location is a given, determined by factors unrelated to their employment. Teenagers, part-time homemakers, and other workers who account for a low proportion of their households' earnings are likely to search for jobs close to their residence. Even if they take positions fairly far from their homes, they may hold them only for limited amounts of time. A large fraction of these workers move in and out of the labor force, depending on labor market conditions and personal circumstances. New jobs going to such workers do not generate new households, but draw on existing ones. More specifically, when a new plant employs such workers, no new household locations result. Our estimate of new households per worker and all household-related costs and benefits should be adjusted downward to take account of this phenomenon.

While this much is clear, the rest of this issue is more uncertain. According to Madden (1981), many two-earner suburban households, knowing the employment location of husbands, choose a residential area with a specific concern for the wives' local job-hunting prospects. Thus, they choose their residential location before the supplementary worker has found a specific job, but their residential choice is not fully independent of job prospects in the area. This scenario means that residential choices may be strongly, even if indirectly, influenced by supplementary job locations.

These considerations suggest that it would be wrong to assume that the job locations of those in multiple-worker households have no effect on where they choose to live. Increasingly, families rely on having two or even more members in the labor force. Deciding where to live has become ever more complex.

In our modeling we take a compromise position: the more significant a worker's earnings to his or her household, the more likely it is that his or her job location is linked to a household's relocation. Only supplementary workers (defined as those contributing less than one-third of household income) have no influence on residential location. Such workers are presumably drawn out of existing populations; hence the jobs they hold lead to no new households in the area.

Overall, we estimate that a new manufacturing plant generates slightly more than one net new household for every two workers. These are households that would not locate in the metropolitan area in the absence of the new facility. Many of these households will be Chicagoans who abandon plans to leave the region once they find employment in the new plant. Others will be drawn from around the country, attracted by specific job opportunities in the new facility. In either case, these are households that would not be in the Chicago area in the absence of plant development.

More specifically, our thousand-worker electrical equipment plant locating in the outer suburbs can be expected to add 524 new households to the Census, while the same plant sited in the central city will add 584 households.[4] The difference is explained by the fact that an outer suburban site is more likely to hire workers from existing households. A disaggregation of the net difference in the number of new households by income level demonstrates that all of the difference occurs, as expected, among low-income households. Indeed, the outer suburban plant actually generates a few more middle- and high-income households than the city plant.

Workers from low-income city households are more likely to take jobs in city firms than in outer suburban ones. As the manufacturing job base of the city has eroded, these households have often had to leave the metropolitan area and/or rely on transfer payments. Locating our electrical equipment plant in the central city will help maintain these households. If, on the other hand, our electrical equipment plant is placed in the outer suburbs, it will draw more heavily on secondary workers from medium- and high-income households. Thus the prosperity of two- and three-earner suburban households will come in part at the expense of low-income central city jobholders.

What will become of the low-income city households that are displaced if our plant chooses a greenfield location? They may well move out of the area in search of better job opportunities. From a narrow regional perspective, this may be a gain—one less low-income household to subsidize. But for the country as whole, the problems associated with the poverty of the low-skilled will not disappear. The costs of providing welfare, schooling, and other social services for these households will simply be borne elsewhere rather than in Chicago. In assessing the effects of locating the electrical equipment plant in the outer suburbs rather than the central city, we must take account not only of differences in household location within the metropolitan area, but also of the households which under one or the other scenario locate outside the region.

Spread Effects

Where a plant locates has an effect not only on its own workers, but on others as well. Bringing a new manufacturing plant to a metropolitan area will expand a host of other economic activities in the area. The plant itself is likely to draw on local suppliers; the workers will spend some of their wages in the metropolitan area. These expenditures, or multiplier effects, may support new jobs in a broad spectrum of industries. In turn, the workers who take those new jobs and who commute to work will also contribute to traffic congestion; their households will similarly require public services. Just as the multiplier effect spreads the initial stimulus among various regional industries, it also spreads it geographically out from the initial plant site.

Any estimate of the costs and benefits from manufacturing deconcentration must include the impacts resulting from such multiplier effects. To make these estimates, we create simulations using the model of the Chicago metropolitan area developed by George Treyz and his associates at Regional Economic Models Incorporated (REMI). The simulations identify indirect and induced jobs by both industry and location.[5]

In total, about 1.4 indirect and induced jobs are created for every new job at an electrical equipment plant. About half of the indirect and induced jobs are in retail and service industries that tend to locate near the residences of the plant's workforce. Even if the electrical equipment plant locates in Chicago proper, many of the people it hires will be residents of outer suburbs. Accordingly, much of the multiplier effect—about 45% of the indirect and induced jobs—will be located in the outer suburbs. Not surprisingly, the workers holding those outer suburban jobs are also likely to live in the suburbs.

In a similar fashion, if the plant locates in the outer suburbs, a more modest but not trivial stimulus will be felt in the city economy. Although few of the plant workers will live in Chicago, the plant will draw on the city for a range of inputs, such as financial and insurance services. It may also purchase intermediate goods from city producers. In fact, about 20% of the induced jobs created by an outer suburban plant will be located in the city.

Altogether, then, whether the new plant locates in the central city or in the outer suburbs, its multiplier effects will be felt widely throughout the metropolitan area. To a great extent, this spreading of multiplier effects testifies to the economic interdependence among the region's industries. Banking and finance continues to be centered in Chicago proper, and even outer suburban manufacturers turn to the city for these services. At the same time, because of decentralization of residence and the extensive commuting between city and suburbs, retailing and other population-serving industries are increasingly moving to the suburbs.

Because of this diffusion of economic activity through the multiplier process, the residential pattern of all new workers (including those holding indirect and induced jobs) will be somewhat less geographically concentrated than for the original manufacturing workers alone.[6] Just as for the initial manufacturing workers, these indirect and induced jobholders will in general be associated with less than one net new household. The point is especially true for low-paying retail and service activities. Such jobholders will often contribute only modestly to the incomes of their households and will have little impact on household residential location.

For workers in indirect and induced jobs, much as for workers in the plant itself, only about one new household will appear for every two jobs. Indirect and induced jobs in the outer suburbs will generate new households at a slightly lower rate. As with direct jobs, this is because outer suburban workers are more likely to be secondary wage earners; thus they are more likely to choose their place of residence first and their place of work for convenience. This is particularly true for workers in low-wage jobs.[7]

A Base for Analysis

The data presented so far have been two-dimensional at most. For example, figure 2-1 shows where manufacturing workers live, given the locations of their jobs. But not every cost or benefit can be neatly linked to only one or two demographic markers. To return to our standard example, the use of public transportation and hence the externality of congestion vary with virtually all of the worker characteristics mentioned so far: workplace location, residence location, household income, and gender. A realistic simulation of commuter behavior must incorporate all of these characteristics.

The calculations we performed rested on such an approach. To simulate the siting of the plant in the central city and the siting in the outer suburbs, we began with estimates from the REMI model of the number of new workers by industry and location. We then divided these workers according to the actual characteristics of real city and suburban workers included in the Census's 1990 Public Use Microdata Sample.

For example, suppose the REMI model indicates that locating the plant in the outer suburbs is likely to generate twenty-five new wholesale jobs in the central city. Who are these people? Where are they likely to live? What are their households like? A REMI simulation alone cannot specify such details. But the PUMS does provide such information—gender, residence, household income, and so on—about current central city workers with jobs such as these. Since the new workers will have similar characteristics, we distribute our twenty-five central city wholesale workers in the same proportions as those suggested by the PUMS for the central city wholesale workers whom it sampled.[8]

At its finest, our simulation divides workers into a total of 540 categories. Each category represents one of all the possible combinations of the ten major industrial categories; the three places of work—city, inner suburbs, and outer suburbs; the three household income levels; and two genders. Since a worker's industry has little relevance to behavior, we drop industry details once we have assigned each worker to a workplace, residence, household income group, and gender. Thus we begin our simulations—one for a central city location and one for an outer suburban location—by allocating all new workers to the fifty-four remaining categories. In a sense, we assign an identity to each worker, typical of similar workers in the real world. On the basis of this identity, we assign behaviors. On the basis of those behaviors, we attempt to estimate social costs and benefits.

Of course, other aspects of workers' identities may also influence the behaviors we model—aspects such as age, race, immigrant status, and size of household.[9] What follows is only a first effort, a starting point emphasizing place of work, place of residence, household income, and gender. Place and income are two characteristics at the heart of the debate over manufacturing deconcentration.

2.3 EXTERNALITIES

For present purposes, we have attempted to identify the most significant externalities associated with greenfield manufacturing locations. Three of these are consequences of automobile transportation: congestion, accidents, and air pollution. Along with trucks, automobiles are the sine qua non of employment deconcentration. Workers in outer suburban manufacturing plants rely almost exclusively on the automobile. In the central city, at least a portion of the labor force uses public transportation. Thus greenfield plant sites will generate greater auto-related costs than central city locations.

In addition, we focus on three other commonly mentioned social costs of peripheral development: loss of open space, the abandonment of city and inner suburban housing, and the underutilization of low-skilled workers in those same areas. As development expands into exurbia, rural open spaces recede farther and farther from the bulk of the metropolitan population. Gains in private land values fail to register the resulting loss in quality of life. As activity moves out from the city center, an even more insidious process occurs in low-income neighborhoods. With thinning populations, property values fall and blight expands, encouraging crime and destroying community feeling. Finally, low-skilled workers in outer suburbs have a greater range of alternatives than workers seeking low-skilled jobs in city and inner suburbs. From the employer's perspective, the wage may be the same or even slightly higher in the city. But from society's perspective, leaving a worker unemployed who has few options represents a real resource cost.

In total, we estimate that locating the plant at a greenfield site rather than a central city one generates an annual loss of approximately $1.1 million in externalities. To connect these estimates to our basic simulations and to clarify the measurement issues they raise, we now consider each in turn.

Congestion

A number of observers have linked the continuing congestion problems of metropolitan areas to the decentralization of jobs into greenfield locations (e.g., MacKenzie, Dower, and Chen, 1992; Downs, 1992; OECD/ECMT, 1995). These analysts emphasize that poorly developed public transit systems in the suburbs make commuting by automobile a virtual necessity. A new outer suburban plant will draw its entire labor force over nearby expressways, highways, and streets.

Yet while it has become commonplace to equate suburban development with traffic congestion, the modern American city has also become dependent on the automobile. Even in Chicago, which has a well-articulated public transit system, a large majority of workers drive to work. Thus we cannot simply assume that a greenfield plant creates greater congestion problems than a city plant; the question must be explored.

Suburban commutes are clearly lengthened by the resistance of many suburbs to balancing their mix of jobs and housing (Cervero, 1989a and 1989b). Some suburban communities remain staunchly residential, sending all of their labor force out onto the highways every morning. More questionable still, major suburban job centers often refuse to allow residential developers to construct housing for low- and moderate-income workers employed in the community.

Of course, each new outer suburban worker makes his or her own decision whether the commute is worthwhile. But every new commuter also imposes costs on those already on the road, thus lessening their quality of life. New city workplace locations will generally impose lower costs.

Still, the issue is not open and shut. A large share of metropolitan traffic runs over the region's spokelike expressways, carrying suburban commuters to central city jobs. Even if the electrical equipment plant locates in the city, many of its workers are already attached to a suburban lifestyle and will opt for a suburban residence.

Do suburban jobs generate more automobile commuting time than city jobs? Ultimately this question can only be answered empirically. Table 2-1, based on the PUMS sample, shows that in the Chicago area almost 95% of all suburban jobholders drive to work, while only 61% of city jobholders drive. When they do drive, city workers are also somewhat more likely to share rides. On the other hand, suburban auto commuters can get to work somewhat faster than city drivers.

The last column in the table provides an index of the contribution of a commuter to metropolitan congestion. The effective auto time per worker measures the (one-way) additional vehicle minutes associated with each type of worker. All things considered, the average suburban worker generates about 30% more vehicle time than does the average city worker.

Of course, the averages presented for workers at city and suburban sites hide considerable variation in behavior. At a more detailed level, table 2-2 presents the summary index of effective auto time for each of the fifty-four worker-groups in our study. Obviously, these effective times are greater for the longer, heavily auto-dependent commutes, whether outer suburb-to-city or city-to-outer suburb. Times are shortest for those who work and live in the same ring, and especially for the city itself, where many commuters use public transit. The effective auto times also vary systematically across our demographic groups. Women have lower times than men. Workers from low-income households have lower times than those from middle- and higher-income households.

These data suggest strongly that a city location will generate less auto congestion than an outer suburban one. The commuting behavior of new workers can be expected to closely mimic that of existing workers. More formally, in our simulations, we attach to each worker the effective auto time for his or her grouping. For example, imagine that the simulation

Table 2-1.

Automobile Commuting Statistics for Workers Employed at City and Suburban Workplaces, Chicago Metropolitan Area, 1990

Workplace	% Commuting by Automobile	One-Way Average Auto Travel Time (in minutes)	Average Number of Riders (in minutes)	One-Way Effective Auto Time per Worker
City	61	29.71	1.30	14.74
Inner Suburbs	93	25.10	1.18	19.76
Outer Suburbs	95	23.01	1.16	18.75

Source: PUMS.

Table 2-2.

Effective Auto Time per Worker for Fifty-Four Worker Types, Chicago Metropolitan Area, 1990

Workplace ⟶	City			Inner Suburbs			Outer Suburbs		
Residence ⟶ Income/Sex	City	Inner	Outer	City	Inner	Outer	City	Inner	Outer
Low/M	10.2	21.3	25.0	18.5	14.9	28.0	24.8	23.8	14.7
Low/W	6.8	16.0	18.1	15.0	13.5	25.6	16.5	21.7	13.6
Mid/M	14.2	23.7	27.2	23.9	18.9	32.3	30.0	28.7	18.6
Mid/W	9.6	17.4	20.6	18.8	14.9	27.1	25.6	23.6	15.2
High/M	13.7	22.6	24.8	24.9	20.0	31.3	35.1	29.9	19.1
High/W	11.0	18.6	21.0	21.6	15.8	27.2	29.8	24.7	15.6

Source: PUMS.

Note: All figures are one-way in minutes.

of a new outer suburban plant projects twenty women from middle-income households, living in the inner suburbs but working in the outer suburbs. Given the data in table 2-2, such workers have an effective auto time of 23.6 minutes each. Aggregating within each scenario across all worker types (including within each type as appropriate both workers in the plant itself and workers filling indirect and induced jobs), we can estimate the difference in auto traffic generated by a central city and outer suburban plant.

The overall results are straightforward. Placing the plant in the central city generates about 47,000 fewer commuting hours per year than locating it in the outer suburbs (331,000 for the city versus 378,000 for the suburbs). While these numbers are closer than some critics of employment sprawl would suggest, they still suggest substantially more traffic with the suburban site than with the central city one. But by themselves, these estimates do not tell the economic value or cost associated with the additional traffic. To put a monetary value on these externalities, we turn to the wealth of literature on the costs of congestion (Small, Winston, and Evans, 1989; Downs, 1992; Mohring and Anderson, 1994).

The basic theory of congestion costs is well known. Commuters who drive are cognizant of their private costs of transport and hence the average cost of their trip. If city dwellers take jobs in distant suburbs and spend three hours a day commuting, presumably they make that choice voluntarily and consider these costs in choosing their residence. But the presence of their vehicles on the road slows down everyone else and thus also imposes costs on others. Even if each additional vehicle slows traffic only a fraction of a minute, it is still interacting with a large number of vehicles, their drivers, and any passengers. The true extra cost to society associated with such congestion can be quite large.

Perhaps no externality has been studied more intensively than congestion costs. For the most part, researchers have multiplied additional time lost in congestion by commuters' value of time, a value usually expressed as fractions of an average wage rate. The resulting figure is then often transformed into dollars per mile. Table 2-3 summarizes the findings of a number of such studies; these estimates are quite consistent with earlier studies of the 1960s and 1970s reviewed by Morrison (1986).

For us, the only serious complication raised by this literature is the work of Pozdena (1988, based on Keeler and Small, 1977). The distinction these authors make between city and suburban highways raises the possibility that commuting trips impose lower costs if they are limited to suburban areas. This result is supported by data from Mohring and Anderson's study of Minneapolis, which suggests that suburban to central city expressways have a per vehicle mile congestion cost close to $0.50, as compared to peripheral interstate costs of about $0.10 to $0.15 per mile.

It is not clear how relevant such estimates are to the Chicago metropolitan area. Given the considerable congestion of Chicago's peripheral highways, there may be less difference between Chicago's city and suburban highways. For example, a recent study of the various tollways in the area concluded that rush hour commutes on the Tri-State Expressway took 40% more time than they would at design traffic flows. Suburban arterial highways were even worse (Aschauer, 1990). Presumably in smaller

TABLE 2-3.

Estimates of Marginal Social Costs of Peak-Hour Traffic

Study	Location	$/Mile
1. Decorla–Souza (1992)	Generic	.30–.55
2. Mohring and Anderson (1994)	Minneapolis	.50 peak urban express
		.10–.15 peak suburban express
3. Pozdena (1988) (Based on Keeler Small [1977])	San Francisco	.80 peak urban highway .25 peak suburban
		.20 fringe road .03–.06 off peak
4. Small, Winston, and Evans (1989)	Summary of British and North America studies	.10–.60 peak

Note: All values converted to 1995 dollars.

metropolitan areas, more easily served by a few interstate highways, the average congestion costs will be lower and the between-suburb commuting will be relatively less than in Chicago. This observations suggests caution in generalizing our congestion findings beyond the largest metropolitan areas.

For Chicago, then, we treat all congestion on an equal footing. Using the data in the above table, we estimate the congestion cost imposed by another commuting vehicle at $0.35 per mile. With an average commuting speed of 30 miles per hour in the metropolitan area, this puts the external cost of an extra peak period vehicle hour at $10.50. The overall value of the congestion externality associated with each scenario is simply this hourly rate times the respective number of commuting hours. This gives an annual congestion cost of $4.0 million for the greenfield plant and $3.5 million for the central city plant—a difference of about $500,000 in favor of the central city location.

In the end, the greenfield site's dependence on intersuburban auto-mobile transport outweighs the long commutes of many suburb-to-city commuters. If the new plant locates in the outer suburbs rather than the central city, existing highway users will find themselves worse off by almost a half million dollars per year.

The Social Costs of Accidents

While highly annoying, congestion is not the only externality created by automobile use. Extra cars also generate more accidents and deaths. Because a greenfield plant produces more suburban households, and because suburban households operate more vehicles, the location of the new plant will affect the number of expected accidents.

To be specific, an average suburban household puts 0.5 more cars on the road than a central city household. Placing the new electrical equipment plant in the outer suburbs rather than the central city brings 250 more vehicles into traffic. This figure would be even larger if it were not for the fact that outer suburban industries draw a greater portion of their labor force from workers supplementing their households' incomes. In the simulation, we do not attribute these workers and their households to the manufacturing plant's site selection. They have not changed their residential locations in response to these opportunities.[10]

While 250 vehicles may not seem like a large number, automobile accidents create such high unpaid costs per vehicle that the difference is significant. At least three studies have attempted to estimate these costs, as summarized in table 2-4.

For these simulations we adopt the MacKenzie, Dower, and Chen estimate because it has a stronger methodological rationale and it lies

TABLE 2-4.

Estimates of Annual Accident Costs Imposed On Others

Study	Location	Per Vehicle
1. DeLuchi in OTA (1994)	U.S.	$937
2. MacKenzie, Dower, and Chen (1992)	U.S.	$425
3. Hanson (1992)	Madison	$207

Note: All values converted to 1995 dollars.

between the two other estimates. MacKenzie, Dower, and Chen start from an Urban Institute (1991) study of the total costs of motor vehicle accidents. This total cost is a broad-based estimate including lost wages as well as household production, medical costs, pain, suffering, and lost quality of life. Observing that 17% of all motor vehicle fatalities are pedestrians and bicyclists (National Safety Council, 1990), MacKenzie et al. consider only this share of the total costs of accidents as an externality. They also adjust the resulting figure downward, since nonmotorists bear little if any of the property damage associated with accidents.[11]

Multiplying this figure by the number of automobiles induced under the two alternative scenarios gives estimates of expected annual accident costs: $1.1 million for the greenfield location and $1.0 million for the central city location, with a difference of about $100,000 per year in favor of the city location. This figure gives the net accident cost associated with the greenfield site.

Air Pollution

Automobile traffic generated by the new plant will also add to the air pollution problems of the metropolitan area. Like the cost of additional accidents, the cost of incremental air pollution depends on the number of new vehicles on the road. The challenge is deciding how to monetize the dollar value of the air pollution created by each vehicle.

To do this, we consult the same three major summaries (see table 2-5) (DeLuchi in OTA, 1994; MacKenzie, Dower, Chen, 1992; Hanson, 1992). The latter two studies arrive at quite similar estimates, each representing a summary of several earlier but not identical studies. DeLuchi's result—actually his low estimate—attempts to measure a much broader set of impacts, including a controversial assessment of deaths due to air pollution. Taking a conservative position, we use MacKenzie, Dower, and Chen's figure of $71 per year per vehicle.

Multiplying this figure by the number of induced vehicles under each scenario gives an estimate of the air pollution costs involved: $178,000 for

TABLE 2-5.
Estimates of Automobile Pollution Costs Imposed On Others

Study	Location	Per Vehicle
1. DeLuchi in OTA (1994)	U.S.	$284
2. MacKenzie, Dower, and Chen (1992)	U.S.	$ 71
3. Hanson (1992)	Madison	$ 76

Note: All values converted to 1995 dollars.

the greenfield site and $160,000 for the city site, yielding a difference of $18,000 per year. If these calculations are correct, alternative plant sitings have relatively similar effects on metropolitan air pollution. However, if the average figures used per vehicle are gross underestimates, then these costs could mount. Such a result would be much more likely in an area such as Los Angeles. Chicago, with its open topography and frequent winds, makes a rather poor case for a linkage between suburban sprawl and air pollution costs.

On the other hand, this result in no way undermines the logic of trying to reduce automobile dependence as a strategy in fighting air pollution. The problem is that so many city jobs are held by suburban automobile commuters. Beyond these drivers, even city residents holding city jobs are likely to use automobiles for commuting, shopping, and recreation. Thus significant reductions in air pollution can be obtained only if all drivers are lured out of their cars. While this may be easier for those who live and work in the city, simply locating more jobs there will not automatically result in the desired behavioral shift.

The Value of Open Space

By definition, suburban sprawl means that farmland and other open spaces in the metropolitan area are replaced by urban residential, commercial, and industrial uses. Presumably, the farm family who voluntarily sells its fields has already included in its price any loss it associates with this transformation. But the loss of greenfields may generate significant externalities as city and suburban residents find themselves ever farther removed from open lands. Many people enjoy a drive in the country or just a sense of proximity. But can one place a dollar value on such feelings? When yet another company builds a new greenfield plant, what losses are imposed on those who formerly enjoyed the openness of that site?

We start with a rather straightforward question: How much greenfield land is absorbed by the type of large manufacturing development under consideration? Such a development also entails spread effects. Besides the initial plant site, how many acres will it cause to be channeled into residential, commercial, and other related developments? Finally, we turn to the much more difficult question: How much is the metropolitan population willing to pay to preserve each of these acres of open space on the urban fringe?

Given recent industrial developments in the Chicago metropolitan area, we expect the electrical equipment plant to directly use 50 acres, or 0.05 acre per employee. As for the various secondary business activities that the plan generates, including industrial suppliers and firms serving the consumption demands of the plant's workforce, much of this new activity will also be located in the outer suburbs and will also encroach on open spaces. Indeed, these new nonresidential uses will themselves absorb about 67 acres of open land.[12]

But there is still more. While the greenfield plant will hire many people who are already living in the suburbs, a large proportion of the new jobs will go to people who will move to the outer suburbs from the city, the inner suburbs, or outside the region. By the very nature of the outer suburbs, these new households can only be situated on formerly open lands.

Residential expansion absorbs more land per worker than does industrial expansion. Of course that absorption will itself differ, depending primarily on the income level of new households. Even in the outer suburbs, two-thirds of low-income households live in multifamily dwellings, each of which absorbs on average only 0.05 acres. By contrast, more than two-thirds of middle-income households and an even larger share of high-income households can be expected to choose single-family homes. In the outer suburbs, such homes absorb an average of 0.25 acres apiece. Taking these differences into account, the estimated 796 new outer suburban households will absorb 241 acres in residential land. This gives a total land absorption by industrial, commercial, and residential expansion of 358 acres.

But this still is not all. Neither the residential nor the nonresidential figures include land for sidewalks, roadways, parks, and other public activities. For low-density suburbs, a reasonable estimate for such uses is 33% of all developed land (Downs, 1992, appendix C). Adding these necessary uses raises the total to 537 acres. In short, the initial 50-acre greenfield industrial site ultimately absorbs more than 10 times that amount of open space.

What happens if the company picks a central city location instead? At first it might seem that no open space would be lost. But this would be true only if none of the new workers chose to live in the outer suburbs. In fact, many of these workers, and especially many of the more prosperous ones with a taste for land-extensive homes, will pick outer suburban residences. In addition, they will be joined by some of the workers who obtain jobs in secondary employment associated with the new plant.

We estimate that the 261 outer suburban resident households predicted under the central city scenario will absorb 86 acres of open space in residential development. When related commercial, industrial, and public uses are added, a new central city plant, somewhat paradoxically, results in the absorption of a total 156 acres of open space.

This result is a testimonial to the strong attraction of the suburbs under current conditions in metropolitan areas. Just as central city development does not guarantee short commutes, in itself it cannot stop the transformation of farmland into suburban land uses. As long as many central city workers seek out suburban residences, city development will contribute to the demise of open spaces. Nevertheless, the greenfield site still results in the absorption of considerably more land than the city site.

Outer suburban residents, even those who only recently moved from the central city, are concerned that the character of their communities is changing. The development of strip malls, the expansion of the highway system, and the spread of new homes force the continuing retreat of open lands. Central city residents, too, may regret these changes in metropolitan form, as they must travel farther and farther to reach rural areas.

How much is this loss of open space worth to metropolitan residents? Can we put a dollar figure on it? The task here is considerably more difficult than in the case of congestion. Lands kept in agriculture and other very low-density uses provide a positive externality to metropolitan residents. The private land market will not generally reflect this public demand for open space. When private developers convert open space to higher-density uses, there is no price in the system to make clear the loss of externalities resulting from their action.

Two possible exceptions to this conclusion should be noted. First, preferential treatment of farmland for property tax purposes implies a subsidy for maintaining land in agricultural uses. Second, public and nonprofit bodies can purchase open lands to guarantee an amenity enhancement of the metropolitan area. In some states these purchases can be of so-called development rights and hence allow land to remain in agriculture.

Perhaps, then, at one extreme it might be argued that ample public and quasi-public mechanisms for maintaining open space already exist. If these mechanisms are not being used more aggressively, one might conclude that the remaining externalities from open space are not that large. Such a conclusion represents an important empirical challenge to those who suspect that open space externalities are large; this challenge has been taken up by several researchers.

The empirical evaluation of the amenity value of farmland and other open spaces has become a serious research effort only with the development of contingent evaluation methodologies in cost-benefit analysis. These techniques use a survey approach to ascertain an individual's willingness to pay for the preservation of open space. While subject to some controversy, contingent evaluation methods have recently won wider acceptance from the economics profession and the law courts (see Portney, 1994; Hanemann, 1994; Diamond and Hausman, 1994).

We have seen only three contingent valuation studies of amenity benefits of open land (Beasley, Workman, and Williams, 1986; Bergstrom, Dillman, and Stoll, 1985; Halstead, 1984). More recently, Lopez, Shah, and Altobello (1994) reworked the data from these studies and estimated "marginal amenity benefits" in dollars per acre per year. They fit a function to the data for the various contingent valuation studies; this function relates the overall value of the farmland amenity (as measured in the various studies) to the population-to-farmland ratio of an area and its per capita income. Having done that, the authors determined the marginal amenity benefit of an acre of farmland in various areas. These values ranged from a low of $12 per acre per year in 1995 dollars for Deerfield, Massachusetts, to a high of $103 per acre per year for East Longmeadow, Massachusetts.

Given the small number of existing studies, it is difficult to measure precisely where the outer suburbs of Chicago would fit into the range defined above. Deerfield is a largely rural area, while East Longmeadow is more dense; both have relatively high per capita incomes. Chicago is a much more highly urbanized area than any of those in Lopez et al.'s study. Apart from possible differences in preferences, this also raises questions over the appropriate geographic area to be considered in the analysis. Presumably, open space at a greater distance is of less value than that at a closer distance.

In a tentative extrapolation, we use Lopez et al.'s formula with approximate values for the Chicago area. The key variable is the number of people in the area per acre of agricultural land. Rough calculations for the Chicago metropolitan area suggest a population per acre of agricultural land approximately twice that for East Longmeadow. This would result in an increase in the marginal amenity benefit by a factor of 1.75, to $180 per acre per year in 1995 dollars.

The 500 and some acres of open land absorbed by the greenfield plant and related developments generate an annual loss of about $97,000. If the plant locates in the city of Chicago, it will still create a cost of $28,000 per year on the 156 acres absorbed. This gives a net difference of $69,000 per year imposed by greenfield development.

Housing Abandonment

Housing abandonment is a serious problem in the central city and many inner suburbs. Abandoned structures tend to deteriorate rapidly and easily become the focus for drugs and crime—obvious social costs. Even a reasonably well-maintained courtyard apartment building becomes far less desirable when another structure on the block is abandoned.

Economic redevelopment slows abandonment by raising incomes and hence increasing the demand for the existing housing stock. Redevelopment's positive impact on the poor and the near-poor translates into fewer abandoned units. Our approach to measurement starts from the proposition that in the city and inner suburbs the ratio between the proportion of the population in poverty and the proportion of housing units abandoned remains approximately constant. Hence if we can determine the number of city and inner suburban residents redevelopment raises out of poverty, we can estimate the reduction in abandonment as well. We can then turn to the literature on abandonment to calculate the dollar cost each abandoned unit imposes on the community. To carry out this evaluation, thus, requires three empirical inputs: the ratio of abandoned units to poverty households, the numbers of city and inner suburban poverty households saved from poverty by the alternative plant locations, and the dollar externality imposed by an abandoned housing unit.

In large cities, roughly 4% (3%–5%) of the housing stock is abandoned (Mills and Hamilton, 1989, p. 223). About 15% of the households in these cities are officially defined as poor. The ratio of abandoned units to poverty households is then about 27%.It seems reasonable to assume that abandonment will move up or down roughly in this proportion to poverty. Abandonment is less likely if very low-income families increase their earnings enough to afford housing of stable quality. If they are renters, they can afford to pay enough rent to induce landlords to maintain their dwellings in reasonable condition. In this situation, the household enjoys a private benefit, the landlord enjoys a private benefit, and society gains as well if the housing unit escapes abandonment.

While abandonment is a serious problem in the central city or inner ring of suburbs, outer suburbs generally have growing population bases, which imply that even low-income housing markets are tight. Hence, even in the absence of a particular development they are not likely to experience housing abandonment. Even if poor households in the outer suburbs do reside in poorly maintained units, the low densities of these communities imply that this process is unlikely to impose sizable externalities.

Given the relationship between household poverty and housing abandonment, it is clear that a new plant should be able to reduce the rate of abandonment. But how many of the jobs at a new plant actually allow a household to stay out of poverty? The PUMS sample allows us to address this question, since it connects individual occupations and earnings to household incomes and family size. If we know a worker's wages and his or her household's income, we can get a good idea of their circumstances in the absence of a particular employment opportunity.

Which scenario keeps more central city and inner suburban households out of poverty?[13] Not surprisingly, when the initial plant is sited in the central city, it scores better on this measure. On net, the city plant maintains 170 more central city and inner suburban households above poverty. (See appendix A1.1.) Multiplying this difference by 27% (derived above) implies that a greenfield development results in forty-six more housing abandonments than a central city siting.

How do we put a dollar value on this externality? Abandonments clearly present a direct loss to their owners. Such costs are not addressed here, but are considered together with land appreciation resulting from development in the section on private benefits and costs. Here our focus is on the external effects of abandonment on the value of nearby properties.

Housing economists have generated a large body of work on the value of neighborhood quality (see, for example, the extensive review by Follain and Malpezzi, 1980). However, we know of only one study that explicitly includes a measure of housing abandonment, that of Ihlanfeldt and Martinez-Vazquez (1986). In a study of Atlanta with the market price of housing units as the dependent variable, they find that "abandoned housing on street" reduces value by approximately 10%.

Using this estimate, the value of eight neighboring properties each worth $25,000 can be expected to fall $20,000 in aggregate as the result of an abandonment. This is a capital loss to the owners of properties near an abandoned unit. Since all other costs and benefits in this study are annual flows, we annualize this figure by taking a loss of 5% per year on the lost capital value, or about $1,000 per year per abandoned unit. This figure is meant to represent the decline in quality of life that is capitalized into the value of these neighboring units.

In total, then, the central city plant and related development generate a stream of improved neighborhood conditions worth $75,000 per year, while the outer suburban plant produces a stream of only $29,000 per year.[14] The difference—$46,000 per year—is a net cost of greenfield development.

Housing abandonment and declining neighborhood quality are serious social costs to central cities and inner suburbs. One might expect that expanding central city manufacturing employment would contribute significantly to reducing these costs. At the margin, however, this does not seem to be the case. Only a modest share of new jobs go to those who would otherwise be in poverty. More critically, each such new job contributes only a small amount per year to the reduction of abandonment. However, as we explain in the next section, whatever the fate of the housing stock, low- and moderate-income households do gain substantially from even these modest employment opportunities.

Underemployment and the Spatial Mismatch of Jobs

The drift of more and more jobs to outer suburban areas, coupled with the concentration of low-income households in the central city and some inner suburbs, gives rise to spatial mismatch in the labor market (Kain, 1968; Wilson, 1987; Kasarda, 1988; Blackley, 1990; Ihlanfeldt and Sjoquist, 1990; Holzer, Ihlanfeldt, and Sjoquist, 1994). This spatial mismatch contributes to the unemployment and underemployment of low-skilled workers in the city. Such unemployment represents a real resource cost of the existing spatial pattern of metropolitan development.

If the new plant locates in the outer suburbs, many of its low-skilled jobs will go to secondary or tertiary workers from middle- or high-income households who have real alternatives. If the plant locates in the city, a higher proportion will go to primary workers from low-income households who have few if any alternatives. This difference is key to the mismatch argument.

In a prosperous economy with low unemployment rates and well-functioning labor markets, workers face a range of job opportunities. If a worker is not employed at job x, he or she will likely find employment somewhere else at about the same wage rate.[15] Economists describe this situation as one in which the "opportunity cost" of labor is roughly equal to the wage.

In contrast to this positive picture, low-wage workers from low-income households face a restricted set of opportunities. Given limited household resources, these workers have few options. Indeed, in the absence of new jobs, they may well be involuntarily unemployed. Even if alternative employment is obtained, it may be part-time or irregular. Determining the opportunity cost of such workers is extremely difficult. Boardman et al. (1996, p. 74) suggest a minimum figure of 50% for unemployed workers. In the absence of a more precise estimate, we adopt this figure for our low-wage–low-income workers.[16] Putting these workers into steady jobs raises production $2 for every $1 of real opportunity cost.

Where do low-wage workers from middle- or high-income households fit into this picture? We argue that they should be treated as average workers with opportunity costs about equal to their wages. Drawing on the resources of more prosperous households, these workers can generally find meaningful alternatives to any specific job. These may take the form of related job opportunities or alternatives to employment—opportunities for work at home, study, or constructive consumption. If such a worker fails to get a specific job, his or her loss will be significantly mitigated by the presence of substantial alternatives. In the absence of more specific information, we use an opportunity cost of 100% for low-wage workers from middle- and high-income households.

Conditional on these estimates, a given low-skilled job employing a worker from a higher-income household as opposed to one from a low-income household creates a real welfare loss. As long as the worker from the more prosperous household has a greater opportunity cost than the worker from the less advantaged household, society does better to allocate the job to the more disadvantaged worker.

City plants hire more low-wage workers from low-income households, many of them primary wage earners. Suburban plants hire more low-wage workers from middle- and high-income households, most of them secondary or tertiary wage earners. Under the circumstances, then, a suburban location creates a real mismatch cost.[17]

In operationalizing these observations, we again turn to the PUMS data. Siting the plant in the central city leads to the employment of 319 low-wage workers from low-income households.[18] Recall that many of these workers will not be employed in the plant itself, but in secondary economic activities such as retailing stimulated by the demands of the plant and its labor force. In contrast, siting the plant in the outer suburbs employs only 245 low-wage–low-income workers, for a difference of 74.

Using these estimates and taking an average annual income of $10,000 per year in 1989 dollars or $12,300 in 1995 dollars, we calculate that a suburban site, relative to a city one, results in a wage loss to low-wage workers from low-income households of $911,000 per year. Against this loss, these same workers have alternative opportunities estimated at 50%, leaving a net loss of $456,000 per year.[19] Notice, the gain in wages achieved by low-wage workers from more affluent households is not included in the calculation since their foregone opportunities are taken to be of approximately equal value.

Only a small share of the more than 2,400 jobs created by the plant affect the level of mismatch. For the most part, new jobs in either city or suburb attract workers away from existing activities in the region or outside. And of course, even the outer suburban plant generates some low-wage jobs for workers from low-income households. Nevertheless, the measured mismatch effect of a greenfield site looms large among the externality costs considered here.

Externalities Outside the Region

A full national reckoning of the difference between an outer suburban and central city location must take account of any externalities imposed or avoided outside the region as the result of differences in household mobility under the two cases. The Chicago metropolitan area is a net exporter of population to the rest of the country. The expansion of employment, whether in the city or the outer suburbs, slows this net outflow and any costs it imposes on other communities.

As we have seen, when a new manufacturing plant chooses a central city location over a greenfield site, it draws more heavily on low- and moderate-income households. These new jobs keep these households in the metropolitan area, preventing them from joining the stream of out-migrants searching for employment elsewhere.

While an outer suburban site holds more middle- and high-income households in the region (seventy more), it keeps fewer low- and moderate-income ones (ninety fewer).[20] As we have seen, households of different income levels produce different externality patterns. High-income households drive more cars, absorb more space, and overall generate more external costs. Even though the greenfield site results in more households locating elsewhere, these households are on average poorer and hence likely to generate fewer externalities (although as we will see in the next section, they generate greater public costs).

The net effects are not large. For example, consider the differences between simulations of the likely congestion experienced outside the metropolitan area. The greenfield plant siting results in a net flow of low-income households to the rest of the country. Using data drawn from our study of transportation patterns in Chicago, we estimate that these households will generate a congestion externality on the rest of the nation of $147,000 per year. At the same time, however, the rest of the nation avoids housing middle- and high-income households who otherwise would have generated more vehicle hours and a congestion cost of $196,000. The rest of the country has a net savings, under greenfield development, of $49,000 in congestion costs.

Similar calculations can be undertaken for the other automobile-related externalities. These result in even smaller net savings for the rest of the country under greenfield development in Chicago, while the savings in open space are trivial.

On the other side, neither the abandonment nor mismatch externalities that favor central city redevelopment are shared with the rest of the country. These externalities are only a function of locating the plant in the Chicago metropolitan area and have no effects outside that area. Assuming that low- and moderate-income households will not on average improve their economic situation by migrating, there is no reason to credit the rest of the country with any positive externalities from absorbing these Chicago out-migrants.

To sum up these externalities, the rest of the nation actually benefits modestly as the result of the outer suburban plant location, avoiding approximately $63,000 of externalities annually. This simply means that if the plant chooses a greenfield site on the fringe of Chicago, some higher-income households clog the expressways in that area rather than elsewhere in the nation.

Externalities: A Summary

Table 2-6 provides a summary of the major externalities related to the plant site decision. The largest externality of greenfield development is congestion, with the closely related category of accidents in third place. For years now, the rapid development of outlying suburbs has left traffic in these growing communities in a state of gridlock. Of course, not all the problem is due to new greenfield plants; many outer suburbanites work in the central city or inner suburbs. But new plants do add to the already congested traffic. A plant that chooses a central city site as opposed to a greenfield site takes pressure off the system—a significant incentive for suburban residents to encourage brownfield development in the central city.

The second largest and perhaps most troubling externality associated with choosing outer suburban development rather than central city redevelopment is caused by the spatial mismatch between low-skilled jobs and low-income households. This result is consistent with the widely held view that central city redevelopment can make a real contribution

TABLE 2-6.

Annual Externalities Generated by New Electrical Equipment Plant

	New Cost of Outer Suburb Siting Relative to Central City Siting
1. Congestion	493
2. Accidents	105
3. Air pollution	18
4. Open space	68
5. Housing abandonment	46
6. Mismatch	426
7. Rest of country	(63)
Total externalities	1121

Note: All figures in thousands of 1995 dollars; ( ) indicates benefit.

to the welfare of low-income households while mobilizing resources that otherwise would be idle. In a real sense, this is what the city population has to gain from brownfield development.

The other three categories—open space, housing abandonment, and air pollution, in order of importance—all favor a city location but represent relatively modest costs to society. While suburban sprawl is often identified with the destruction of open space and the environment, it doesn't seem, at least for the time being, that metropolitan residents are very concerned about these losses.

Taken together, $1.1 million annual negative externalities are real costs or foregone benefits that accumulate to members of society, who have little say in choosing the plant's location. These costs represent a loss—foregone production or value lost if the plant locates in the outer suburbs.

In addition to such real losses imposed directly on individuals, the location of the plant generates a series of significant costs through the public sector. Many of these are borne by the taxes of the new suburban residents and firms, but many others are subsidies from higher levels of government or existing suburban taxpayers. A full reckoning of the costs of greenfield development requires consideration of these public subsidies as well.

2.4 PUBLIC-SECTOR COSTS

Manufacturing location decisions have important implications for public costs. Where a plant locates affects local government budgets, highway construction, and even federal tax revenues. As this section shows, a greenfield location for our electrical equipment plant generates $1.5 million more in public costs than a central city location. Almost half these costs originate in losses by local governments.

These public costs are clearly transfers in favor of suburban residents. In general, a transfer of a dollar from one person to another does not necessarily imply that efficiency is lost or that the size of the overall economic pie is reduced. But in this case, these transfers do in practice result in real resource losses to the economy at large. To explain this claim, we begin by considering the local fiscal losses associated with greenfield development.

Local Fiscal Impacts

Households and businesses locating in the outer suburbs generally pay lower taxes and receive public services of equal or higher value than similar households and businesses in the central city. Lower local taxes are often a major reason why firms choose outer suburban locations; fiscal flight has long been a reality of American metropolitan life. This fact has important distributional implications. As more and more businesses and their employees move out of the city, the implicit redistribution achieved through the provision of local services is threatened.

The ability of businesses and more affluent households to avoid redistributive taxation raises important ethical questions. Many critics of American suburbanization have argued that it enables suburbanites to shirk their responsibility for the urban poor. While such distributional issues are fundamental to local public finance, our major concern here is with social costs and efficiency. Apart from equity implications, how does the flight from city taxes create an efficiency loss?

The nation as a whole sacrifices efficiency and wastes resources whenever it uses a more expensive method than necessary to achieve its current level of well-being. If the same result can be achieved more economically, then an inefficiency exists. In this context, consider two households with similar tastes enjoying the same level of well-being. One of these households lives and works in the city where, through its local taxes, it makes a considerable contribution to the support of the poor. The other lives and works in the outer suburbs, where it makes a much smaller contribution. If, as hypothesized, the two households enjoy the same level of well-being, then we have found a genuine inefficiency. Under these circumstances, the difference between the city and outer suburban households' contributions measures a real loss or cost to society associated with the outer suburban household.

This argument suggests an empirical approach to measuring real public-sector costs under alternative plant locations. These costs can be approximated by the difference in the net (additional revenue minus additional expenditures) local fiscal contributions between the two cases. As suggested above, this approach holds only if the households being compared actually enjoy the same level of well-being. How can we be sure that two households in two different scenarios are enjoying the same welfare level?

If the plant locates in the central city, some of its workers live in the city, some live in the suburbs. If the plant locates in the outer suburbs, more workers will locate in the suburbs. Under either scenario the residential location of some households will remain "fixed." These households are committed in terms of their residential choices. Their taxes and public services are determined without reference to the plant's location. They do not enter into our calculation of changes in local public costs and expenditures. But there is a major group of households whose taxes and public services differ under the two scenarios. These are the ones that choose to locate in the city if the plant is located there and in the suburbs if the plant locates there.[21] We claim that these "mobile" households, controlling for broad income levels, enjoy about the same level of well-being under the city scenario as under the outer suburban one.

Urban economic theory suggests that such mobile households should be enjoying virtually identical well-being under the two scenarios. If this were not the case—if, for example, the outer suburban scenario leaves them appreciably better off than the city scenario—then they would have a major incentive to seek both employment and housing in the suburbs under either scenario. If both labor markets and housing markets function reasonably well, these mobile households should be close to indifferent between working/living in the city and working/living in the suburbs. Hence they should be just about indifferent between their outcomes under the two scenarios.[22]

In some sense, these mobile households, making a relatively large net fiscal contribution under the city scenario, are just as happy as they would be under the outer suburban scenario with a lower contribution. That difference is an element of the efficiency loss associated with the outer suburban location. The change in the fiscal surplus (or deficit) from one simulation to the next gives a measure of the overall efficiency loss associated with the public sector. In this section we estimate the differences in these fiscal surpluses.

A few points of clarification may be helpful. Unlike some popular analyses of these issues, we do not suggest that the bottom line is simply the cost of the new public infrastructure needed in the case of a siting in the outer suburbs. It is not always wasteful to desert old capital and build new capital. As a number of urban economists have suggested, higher income levels may well lead to a taste for lower densities. As such, the new public capital may make possible a real increase in welfare. The fact that the expansion of fringe communities requires a new $4 billion highway in itself does not mean that suburbanization wastes resources; the cost of the highway must be weighed against the increase in welfare it will bring. If the new residents prefer a low-density lifestyle, they may feel that their welfare gains are greater than the cost of the highway.

The measure of inefficiency in greenfield development is not its total price, but the extent to which such development requires external subsidies to offset that price. The general research consensus is that residential development may fall short of paying its way, and that low- or moderate-income residential development probably falls far short (Oakland and Testa, 1995; Burchell and Listokin, 1995).

Residential Impacts

The net local fiscal contribution of a household depends on both the taxes it pays and the costs of the public services it consumes. For the most part, the taxes falling on a new household just equal the average taxes paid by similar households already in the community. Expenditures, however, are considerably more complicated. In particular, average public expenditure costs may be a poor guide to actual marginal expenditures.

The Census of Governments and related documents give us a rich source on average taxes, fees, and other local revenues, as well as local expenditures. Figures for the Chicago metropolitan area suggest that both average household taxes and expenditures are higher in the city proper than in the outer suburbs. Annual per household local revenues are about $8,500 in Chicago proper and only $5,900 in the outer suburbs. But the difference in these figures greatly overstates the difference in the revenue contribution per household. Chicago businesses contribute a larger share of the local revenue than do businesses in the outer suburbs.[23] Similarly, transfers from state and federal levels of government comprise a somewhat larger share of local Chicago revenues than of outer suburban revenues (29% versus 23%). All told, the difference in average local revenue paid per household is only about $800, or an average 17% savings from a move to the outer suburbs. The figure for the inner suburbs is much closer to that of the city than to that of the outer suburbs.

City households spend more for public services than outer suburban ones. City public services are not cheap. Per household local public expenditures in the city are considerably greater than those in the outer suburbs. Of course, this doesn't necessarily imply that city residents receive more services. In part the difference is the result of the greater concentration of businesses and other nonresidential activities in the city. In addition, older infrastructure, inefficient layouts, higher wages, and larger bureaucratic costs all contribute to the city's higher per household expenditure. After adjusting for public expenditures on nonresidential activities, we estimate that in the Chicago metropolitan area this difference amounts to $1,350 per household.[24] In sum, the average city household requires considerably higher public expenditures than the average outer suburban one. Indeed, the difference more than offsets the corresponding difference in taxes per household.

What is true on average is not necessarily true at the margin. While averages may be a good guide to measuring revenues, they are quite misleading when it comes to expenditures, especially expenditures in the central city. In the outer suburbs, marginal costs are actually likely to be greater than average costs. When households are attracted by new jobs, this necessitates such expenditures as the construction of a new school, an expansion of the police station, and an extension of the sewer system. In sum, servicing new households on the urban fringe requires the expansion of the fixed public capital and new systems of provision. These costs might actually be higher than existing averages, since growth often involves rising input costs.

Outer suburban municipalities have become increasingly aware of the substantial capital costs associated with new residential development. They have sought to recapture some of these expenditures through development impact fees. Currently, impact fees in the most rapidly growing residential areas of the outer suburbs around Chicago run about $10,000 per dwelling. But not all areas are so aggressive. We estimate that impact fees in the outer suburbs average $8,000 per new household. On an annual basis (at 5% per year), this reduces per household marginal expenditures by local government by $400. Taking a relatively conservative approach, we estimate marginal outer suburban expenditures by the existing average less this correction for impact fees.[25]

Outer suburbs have trouble keeping marginal costs imposed by new households in line with existing average costs; older central cities have the opposite problem. Cities like Chicago with declining populations generally find marginal savings from population losses to be far less than would be expected if each departing Chicagoan reduced city costs proportionately. This widely accepted observation implies that such places will find it relatively inexpensive to provide services to new households. Even with high average expenditures, the marginal expenditure in Chicago is actually lower than in the outer suburbs. Overall, we estimate the additional public expenditures per new middle-income household in Chicago to be about $1,250 *less* than the public outlay associated with such a household in the outer suburbs. Taking into account differences in tax and fee payments, this difference in marginal expenditures implies that when such a household locates in the central city rather than the outer suburbs, local governments lose over $2,000 per year. This figure depends critically on our estimates of relatively low marginal costs for various city services. If an employed household moves into Chicago proper, its decision puts little burden on local government. Most of the public departments from which it receives services experience little or no decline in costs when the number of households in the city falls; hence they face little increase when population falls at a slower rate.

For each expenditure category, we have made a rough determination of the ratio of the marginal expenditure in the city to the city average. On the basis of discussions with both academics and public officials, we estimate that a newly employed city household imposes local costs considerably lower than the average. In fact, for some services such as sewerage, a new household imposes virtually no new costs. At the other extreme, an additional city household will generate about 75% of the average per household educational expenditure. Table 2-7 presents our full set of estimates by function. (Note that highway expenditures, with their substantial state and federal subsidies, are considered separately in the next section.)[26]

Of course, the fiscal impact of a household on a jurisdiction varies not only by location but also by income group. On the revenue side, higher-income households contribute more in property and sales taxes than do middle- and low-income households.[27] On the other hand, low-income households in the city use the public school system more intensively than do middle- and high-income households.[28] Taking all these factors into account, we conclude that wherever they locate, higher-income households generate large surpluses, while low-income households result in net costs. However, in the central city, the surpluses of the wealthier are greater, and the costs following the poor are less (see table 2-8).

Several qualifying observations should be restated here. First, we have yet to consider any welfare impacts on workers who have preferences as to the siting of the facility. These will be considered in the discussion of private benefits.

Second, no claim is being made here concerning the relative costs of low- and high-density development. A number of studies suggest that the public costs associated with high-density suburban development are less than those of low-density suburban development (Real Estate Research Corporation, 1974; Burchell, 1992). Other research by Ladd (1992) argues that providing public services in real-world high-density places (as opposed to hypothetical high-density suburbs) is more expensive than in

TABLE 2-7.

Costs Imposed by a New City Household as Share of Average City Costs per Household

0%	25%
Community Development	Administration
Housing	Libraries
Interest	Other Transit (Nonhighways)
Sewerage	Parks and Recreation

50%	75%
Fire	Education
Health and Hospitals	
Police	
Sanitation	

TABLE 2-8.

Annual Net Local Fiscal Impact per New Household by Income
Group and Location

	Chicago	Inner Suburbs	Outer Suburbs
Low income	−220	−1012	−1438
Middle income	1416	−99	−657
High income	5410	3095	2079

Notes: All figures in 1995 dollars.

real-world low-density places. This debate has important ramifications, but it is not central to our present purposes. Clearly, in areas like Chicago, the average costs of public services are higher in the central city than in the suburbs. Again, the estimates presented here relate only to marginal costs in a metropolitan area with a large central city experiencing population losses.

Finally, the estimates presented here do not count state and federal intergovernmental transfers as part of marginal revenues. Subsequently, we will consider the share of these costs associated with highway construction. As for the rest, these transfers allow local expenditures in excess of locally generated revenues, and help offset shortfalls in local budgets. To the extent that such transfers are linked to population, local governments view them as marginal revenues. Even though per capita intergovernmental transfers are relatively larger in the central city, the linkage between population and transfers will be strongest in the growing outer suburbs. Thus, from the perspective of outer suburban local governments, it may be a "paying proposition" to expand the number of middle-income households because of these population-linked transfers.

So much for qualifications. Overall, this discussion of the fiscal impact of marginal population growth in city and suburbs allows us to estimate the public resource cost associated with the residential changes generated by each of our two scenarios. These calculations involve connecting every "new" household, as characterized by its income and residential location, to the appropriate net fiscal surplus.

When the electrical equipment plant is located in Chicago proper, local governments, aggregated across the metropolitan area, will register strong gains in residential revenues. Indeed, these will outweigh public expenditures for new residents by about $680,000 per year. Not surprisingly, the bulk of these gains are realized in the city itself. Under the outer suburban scenario, gains in the inner suburbs and the central city almost offset the considerable costs in the outer suburbs, leaving total residential expenditures for all areas about $20,000 greater than new residential revenues. Thus, the residential fiscal impact of the city scenario bests that of the outer suburban case by about $700,000 per year.

While the city gains the most when the plant locates there, it still gains even if the plant locates in the outer suburbs. The reverse commuters who find employment in the suburbs bring a fiscal surplus back to the city. On the other hand, since new outer suburban households must be modestly subsidized, there are resource costs associated with these areas under both scenarios.

Nonresidential Impacts

Under each scenario, a portion of new local government revenues and new expenditures will be associated directly with businesses and other nonresidential activities. Previous research on such taxes shows that businesses in the suburbs tend to more than pay their way (Oakland and Testa, 1995).[29] If an outer suburban plant is able to make a similar or higher rate of profit than a city one and make a larger net fiscal contribution, that increased contribution, other things being equal, represents an efficiency gain.

On the revenue side, nonresidential property assessments per employee are surprisingly similar in the central city ($9,019) and the outer suburbs ($8,652). We use these as the key link in estimating new revenues, including fees and utilities, per employee. Higher city tax rates yield revenues per employee ($1,267) about twice as high as for the outer suburbs ($609).[30] The inner suburbs end up in between these two ($836).

The net fiscal surplus generated directly by new businesses requires a comparison of these tax revenues per employee with public expenditures per employee. Nonresidential public expenditures per employee are much more difficult to estimate than revenues. As noted above, analysts agree that businesses bring in more revenue than they demand in services. In our surveys of suburban and city planners, no one suggested that nonresidential public services were greater than nonresidential revenues. Nonresidential service requirements may be as little as 40% of the direct revenues such uses generate.

We have little reason to think businesses would be relatively more demanding in the city than in the suburbs, or vice versa; there are arguments on both sides. The density of the central city may raise the cost of providing business services, but the presence of a well-established infrastructure should lower many elements of these costs. A full engineering study of these questions is beyond the limits of the present work.

Under the circumstances, we adopt a neutral course consistent with the consensus that in all areas, businesses more than pay for themselves. In this spirit, our estimates assign a constant ratio of nonresidential expenditures to nonresidential revenues of 60%. This figure roughly agrees with recent research summarized by Altshuler and Gomez-Ibanez (1993). It should be noted that since revenues per employee are higher in the central city, the constant 60% expenditure-to-revenue ratio implies higher expenditures per employee there also.

Using the 60% ratio and the revenues-per-employee figure given above, and working from the basic employment distributions discussed in section 2.2, we can estimate the nonresidential fiscal surpluses under each of our scenarios. The results, an annual surplus of almost $1 million for the central city siting and $750,000 for the greenfield siting, reflect the higher tax rates in the city. The difference is tempered by the spread of secondary employment away from the initial location.

Several researchers (e.g., McGuire, 1987) have hypothesized that fiscal surpluses created by nonresidential land users are implicit payments for externalities imposed by these activities. Our estimates suggest that some rough truth lies in this proposition as it applies to the central city. Here the fiscal contribution from various businesses following on the location of the manufacturing plant in the central city about equals the aggregate externality costs. However, if the plant locates in the outer suburbs, with its higher externalities and lower taxes, the payments fall considerably short of the externalities imposed on society. Indeed, this is a basic part of the problem associated with greenfield development.

Total Local Fiscal Impact

Adding together residential and nonresidential fiscal impacts suggests that locating in the outer suburbs brings about $740,000 into local coffers annually, while locating in the central city generates $1.66 million per year for local governments—a difference of about $925,000 per year. Overall, these results seem consistent with other research. The city has large investments in infrastructure that must be maintained regardless of marginal changes in population and business activity. Additional high-income residents put only a modest burden on the city, while bringing in considerable tax revenues. When the prime facility locates in the city, the overall fiscal impact is substantial. In the outer suburbs, growth in local expenditures is much more closely linked to growth in population and business activity. New facilities generate demand for public services directly and through the new households they attract to the outer suburbs.

Highway Subsidies

Perhaps no aspect of outer suburban development has caused as much controversy as the massive highway construction programs that enable that development. Opponents of sprawl argue that these road-building expenditures are ultimately self-defeating, as every new highway calls forth further waves of road-clogging congestion. Defenders emphasize that the expansion of the highway system simply responds to well-articulated public demands. We have already considered the traffic congestion generated by new development; another question is whether new highway users receive benefits commensurate to the costs of new highway construction.

To begin, we again must distinguish between average and marginal costs. While additional vehicles on city roadways may contribute to congestion externalities, they do not in general entail an expansion of the city transportation system. Faced with a steady or declining population, central cities attempt to maintain existing highway systems. Within broad limits, the bulk of street and highway expenditures in such cities will be undertaken regardless of the level of population and usage. But in the outer suburbs marginal expenditures are quite close to average ones. As the population expands, the system must expand close to proportionately.

From the point of view of efficiency, this simple observation means that any expansion of outer suburban highways represents a real cost to society. But costs can be offset by benefits. To the extent that such expansions are paid for by the users themselves, welfare gains presumably equal or exceed the costs involved. However, to the extent that expansion is financed by net subsidies, the costs accrue without an apparent corresponding gain in welfare.

While subsidies to improve outer suburban highways represent real net costs to society, subsidies for roads that would have existed and required maintenance in any event may represent a transfer rather than a net cost to society. Subsidies of this latter type would be required regardless of declines in the city's population.

As we have shown, whether a plant locates in the city or in the outer suburbs makes a dramatic difference in the number of households that will take up residence in the outer suburbs. Accordingly, while an outer suburban location will generate about 1,600 additional vehicles owned by outer suburban households, a city location will generate only about 600 additional vehicles in the outer suburbs. How large is the subsidy for each of these net new vehicles?

Taking a very conservative approach, we use the average subsidy per vehicle as minimum estimate of the marginal subsidy of each of these outer suburban vehicles. DeLuchi has estimated that nationwide, in 1990 automobile users paid at most $72 billion for highway infrastructure and services, but received somewhere between $103 billion and $136 billion in vehicle infrastructure and services (OTA, 1994). The higher estimate claims a rather implausible police protection subsidy. In any case, we have already included local police services as part of local expenditures in the previous section.[31] Using the lower $103 billion estimate implies a net subsidy of $33 billion in 1990 dollars, or $39 billion in 1995 dollars. MacKenzie, Dower, and Chen (1992) place the corresponding subsidy figure at $34.3 billion ($29.3 billion in 1990 dollars).

With 165 million vehicles on the road nationwide, the slightly more conservative MacKenzie et al. figure implies an average subsidy of $208 per vehicle per year. If each vehicle commuting only in the outer suburbs imposes this cost on other taxpayers, then the greenfield plant placement entails about $210,000 more per year than the city placement. Since, as discussed above, outer suburban households are presumably maintaining only the same level of welfare as similar households in the central city, this figure represents a genuine resource cost to society.

Housing Subsidies

The urban housing stock includes a large proportion of multifamily rental units, while suburban dwellings are far more likely to be single-family. Homeowners gain a considerable tax advantage by owning. Under existing tax laws, the interest payments on mortgages on owner-occupied single-family dwellings are tax-deductible. Many have noted that this favorable treatment of mortgages represents a major tax subsidy encouraging suburban development; as such, it represents a real social cost. As we have argued earlier, if similar households in the city and in the outer suburbs enjoy similar levels of welfare, then other things being equal, the subsidy to outer suburban households must be a real cost necessary to maintain equal welfare levels.

Economists largely agree that deducting mortgage interest in itself does not constitute a subsidy. Interest payments are a cost of doing business, just like those paid by apartment owners. The real difference in tax treatment is that owner-occupants of single-family units are not required to declare the net income they draw in kind from their dwellings. If such a unit were owned by a third party and rented to the household, the rental income less expenses of that third party would have to be counted as taxable income. But when a household "rents" a dwelling to itself, the implicit income earned on its housing investment escapes taxation. The implicit earnings of owner-occupied housing are already included in official estimates of gross domestic product. Several countries recognize the importance of such income and impose taxes on it.

The appropriate measure of housing subsidy, then, requires valuing the tax that would be levied against net income generated by owner-occupied housing if reported. From data in the PUMS, we can determine rates of homeownership and average home values for each income group in each location. We can use these to estimate taxes avoided under each scenario.[32]

Since the outer suburban siting of our electrical equipment plant leads to many more new households living in owner-occupied dwellings, it generates considerably larger subsidies than the central city siting. The net difference is $350,000 per year. We view this difference as a net cost to society of the plant's locating on a greenfield site. Again, we view this as not just a transfer to lucky suburbanites. Rather, if the subsidy enables outer suburban households to maintain roughly the same welfare as their counterparts in the city, then the subsidy represents a real cost. Had these households located in the city, they would be no worse off and society would be better off by the amount of the subsidy.

The Rest of the Nation

As in the case of externalities, the intrametropolitan location of the electrical equipment plant has ramifications for public expenditures outside the metropolitan area. Recall that if the plant locates in the outer suburbs rather than the city, this results in a net increase in middle- and high-income households in the Chicago metropolitan area, while low- and moderate-income households are pushed outside the region. Keeping more higher-income households in the Chicago area means that the subsidies they might receive for highway construction or income taxes foregone have already been counted in the Chicago figures. Since they live in the Chicago area, the flow of such subsidies elsewhere is reduced.

But when it comes to local-sector expenditures, things are very different. Because the rest of the country receives larger numbers of low- and moderate-income households, it must provide greater subsidies to low-income households. At the same time, the rest of the country enjoys lower net surpluses from high-income households.

With these elements working against one another, on net public-sector expenditures of about $62,000 will be generated in the rest of the country pursuant to the electrical equipment plant's location in the outer suburbs of Chicago rather than the central city. Again, the biggest items here are the various subsidies for low-income households funneled through local governments. These are real social costs, because if the plant had located in the central city, these households would have been able to support themselves.

The Public Costs of Greenfield Development

We can now bring together all the public costs associated with choosing the greenfield alternative. If we compare simply the net difference between simulations, we note that the highway subsidies that receive such great attention add only modestly to the total (see table 2-9). Much larger are the nonresidential and residential local fiscal subsidies, amounting to $925,000 per year. These public-sector costs, together with our estimates of externality costs, total more than $3 million annually. This figure provides a comprehensive if somewhat speculative treatment of the social costs of employment decentralization.

To the best of our knowledge, these estimates represent the first attempt to simultaneously measure the externalities and public-sector costs associated with greenfield development. In producing these estimates, we have tried to link business expansion to residential development in line with the realities of metropolitan America. That is, we have not based our analysis on ideas of visionaries, but on how the world is now. Moreover, our method allows us, in principle, to include all costs and benefits, not just those of the particular municipality in which the business development occurs. We have tried to estimate the externalities and public service costs throughout the metropolitan area that would actually follow upon the siting of the model facilities. While the range of uncertainty here is still, unfortunately, large, the message seems clear: employment deconcentration is associated with large unpaid costs and large foregone opportunities.

TABLE 2-9.

Annual Increase in Public-Sector Costs Associated with the Choice of a Greenfield Location Rather Than a Chicago Location

	Net Cost (benefit)
1. Local fiscal losses	
A. Nonresidential	221
B. Residential	704
2. Highway subsidy	211
3. Owner-occupied housing	350
4. Rest of country	62
Total cost to public sector	1548

Notes: All figures in thousands of 1995 dollars.

2.5 PRIVATE BENEFITS AND COSTS

We now turn to private benefits and costs. More specifically, we consider changes in workers' commuting costs and wages, costs to owners of land and structures, and benefits to businesses. Under the latter category fall differences in wage costs, land costs, taxes, and construction costs. Overall, we estimate that private benefits total about $2.6 million more annually in the greenfield case than in the central city case. By far the largest share of these benefits originates in the greater business profits made possible by the lower levels of suburban wages, and especially by the lower levels of women's wages. We consider each benefit category in turn.

Residents

Given all the talk of America's love affair with the suburban lifestyle, one might expect that a greenfield location for a new plant would generate considerable welfare for worker households. In fact, we find evidence of real losses. Of course, many households do enjoy suburban living greatly, but these households can and will live in the suburbs even if their wage earners work in the city. Hence they can extract much of the welfare associated with suburban residence even if the plant locates in the city. The only benefits gained by such workers if their plant takes a suburban location come from reductions in their commuting costs. Moreover, these gains are reduced by the fact that suburban jobs pay lower wages than city jobs. At the same time, workers who actually reverse commute to the suburbs suffer both increased commuting costs and reduced wages.

To make these points clear, consider three groups of worker households: those that will take the same residence and workplace in either case, those that will change both residence and workplace, and those that will keep the same residence but change workplaces.[33] The first of these groups remains in the same situation and hence can have no major change in its welfare. Nor will the second group experience large changes in welfare. This is the group we have already analyzed at some length in our consideration of local fiscal costs. They choose a city residence when their (only or primary) job is in the city, and a suburban residence when it is in the suburbs; they are relatively indifferent to where they live. As we have already argued, their welfare is about the same under both scenarios.

The households that are seriously influenced by the plant's choice of location are those in the third group, who maintain their residential locations regardless of whether their employer locates in the city or suburbs. These committed households gain in reduced commuting costs if their firm chooses a location closer to their place of residence; they lose if it takes one at a great distance. For example, we find that if the plant chooses a greenfield site over a central city site, some 162 outer suburban residents will have significantly shorter commutes. Among the "committed resident" workers, 242 inner suburban residents will also benefit, since for them, commuting to the outer suburbs on average is shorter than commuting to the central city. On the other hand, 102 city residents will make reverse commutes to the outer suburbs and hence suffer a loss in welfare relative to a city site. On net, the outer suburban plant site reduces the commuting time of "committed residents" by about 40,000 hours per year.

What is an hour of commuting time worth to the commuter? In general, workers with higher incomes put a higher price on their time. The transportation literature suggests a value of time in commuting equal to about a third of an individual's wage.[34] With these figures, we estimate that an outer suburban location for the plant brings net welfare increases to committed residents of about $270,000 a year.

The commuting figure favors a greenfield site, because many central city workers already commute from the outer suburbs. Moreover, these commuters tend to have higher than average incomes and hence will value any savings in their commuting time at a relatively high dollar amount. If the plant locates in the outer suburbs rather than the central city, these workers will enjoy gains. On the other side, relatively few central city workers will take a job at a greenfield location without changing residence. For one thing, the wages for many of the unskilled jobs simply would not justify the commute. In addition, some central city workers who might be willing to commute may be discriminated against in the outer suburbs, or made to feel less than welcome. We do not know the commuting preferences of workers subject to such discrimination. To the extent they would choose to reverse commute we may overstate the commuting gains associated with outer suburban locations. And, of course, if discrimination is in some way easier in the outer suburbs, we are also failing to reckon the full social costs associated with that discrimination.

The commuting gains reported here must be weighed against real losses in wages by these "residentially committed" workers. A firm choosing an outer suburban location is motivated in large part by the labor savings obtainable on the periphery of the metropolitan area. As suggested above, "mobile" workers, those who adjust their residence in response to their workplace, enjoy about the same welfare under either scenario. However, in the outer suburbs, the "residentially committed" definitely face lower wages that must be considered in estimates of costs and benefits.

From our discussion of differences in commuting patterns, we already know that about five hundred workers will retain their residence, but alter their workplace from central city to outer suburb should the firm pick the latter site over the former. We also know the income category of these workers. (Again, see note 36.) To estimate their losses at an outer suburban work site, we only need information on quality-adjusted wage differentials between city and suburb. This question is considered in detail in "Businesses: Wage Costs," below. There we find a city–outer suburb differential of 2.4% for men and 9.6% for women. Using these figures, we estimate a wage loss for the residentially immobile of $630,000 per year.

These wage losses to fixed residents outweigh the reduction in their commuting costs. The overall loss amounts to $360,000. We take this to be the private cost to residents.

Land/Structure Owners

In considering the externalities associated with greenfield plant locations, we have observed that residents in the metropolitan area put a value on access to open space. On the other hand, rural to suburban land conversion generates increased market value to landowners. In bidding for attractive locations, new suburban households enrich those who have invested in fringe land. Where suburbs offer attractive amenities and/or subsidized public benefits, landowners will enjoy even more substantial appreciation associated with local growth. Increased land values follow more intensive uses of resources and genuine improvements in efficiency. Critics of suburban sprawl have pointed out the negative externality, while supporters of suburban development have focused on movement of market values.

In the present case, we have no reason to include outer suburban land appreciation in our calculations. Given reasonably well-functioning and flexible land markets, a modest shift of economic activity to the outer suburbs from the central city has no appreciable effect on land values in either location. Presumably, the "next best use" for a parcel of land will always pay about the same price as the actual use. If our plant or residential development hadn't occupied this site, some other activity would have paid essentially the same price. (See appendix A3.) Similarly, in the central city we expect that alternative uses at market prices are readily available for the bulk of released land and released housing capital.[35]

The exception to these observations is generated by housing abandonment. Abandonment forces land and structures into a type of involuntary unemployment. For an extended period of time, abandoned properties lose their market value. We have already noted that our two cases differ in their impact on housing abandonment in the central city and inner suburbs. In particular, the outer suburban site for the electrical equipment plant leads to forty-six more abandonments than the central city siting. Structures saved from abandonment represent a net benefit to their owners. Taking as before each housing unit to have an initial value of about $25,000, we calculate a net direct housing loss of $1.15 million. Annualizing this capital figure at 5% per year gives a loss of $58,000 per year. This approach only counts losses to owners of the most marginal structures. Again, we assume that the market for higher-quality structures in the central city and inner suburbs is not likely to show much movement as the result of modest shifts in demand. These markets, like more skilled labor markets, should be close to clearing. Only the marginal market for the lowest-quality housing represents a discontinuity. In essence, these units, like low-wage, low-skilled workers, can become involuntarily unemployed.

Businesses

Wage Costs

The chief gain to businesses from locating in the suburbs comes in the form of lower wages for labor of equal quality, or—what amounts to the same thing—higher quality for labor at equal wages. Among wage earners with equal levels of schooling and abilities, those working in the outer suburbs will work for less than those in the city. This result is predicted by residential location theory. As a number of urban economists have suggested (Mills, 1972; White, 1976), suburban residents who otherwise would commute to the central city should be willing to accept lower wages in exchange for a reduction in their commuting time. These workers pull down wages in the outer suburbs.

This phenomenon, known as the wage gradient, will be influenced by several factors. As White (1976) argues, extensive suburban development that bids up the value of suburban land will eventually put pressure on suburban wages. In equilibrium, land prices and wage differences just equalize the welfare of mobile households in different locations, but the precise mix of land rent differences and wage differences will depend on the extent of suburban development. At the same time, the gradient depends heavily on the value suburban residents place on commuting time; as noted earlier, the literature on commuting emphasizes the link between wage levels and the value of commuting time. However, another major influence in this area is the individual's responsibilities for home production and child care. More specifically, it seems that because women on average carry more of these responsibilities, they put high value on their commuting time (Dubin, 1991). Dubin concludes that women follow the monocentric model, with its emphasis on the cost of commuting, more closely than men. This finding is consistent with the PUMS data, which show that for almost all household income levels and residential locations, women workers spend less time commuting than their male counterparts.

Motivated by such observations, we set out to measure the relevant wage differences for men and women in city and suburbs. To estimate separate wage equations for men and women, we included the following independent variables: place of work, race, education, age, U.S. birthplace, English-language household, disability status, part-time status, military service, marital status, and twenty-two occupational dummies. The dependent variable is the natural logarithm of the individual's hourly wage as estimated from the PUMS.[36] Because of the large sample size, virtually all the coefficients in these equations are significant.

The standard variables such as education all have the expected signs suggested by the labor economics literature.[37] Being black or Hispanic represents a cost to the individual; being a black male has an especially high cost, about 15%. Interestingly, being married raises men's wages significantly but has no effect on women's wages. Having children lowers the wages of both men and women by about 10%. The coefficients on age and the square of age suggest that the wages of both men and women peak at about 50 years old. Our most interesting finding here is the significant reduction in wages at workplaces in the suburbs. For men, this reduction is less than 1.5% in the inner suburbs, less than 2.5% in the outer suburbs. For women the effect is considerably larger: about 7% in the inner suburbs and 10% in the outer suburbs. These estimates strongly support the hypothesis that businesses pay lower wages for labor of a given quality in suburban locations.

Because the place-of-work coefficients were so large for women workers, we explored the wage equation for women in more detail. When we broke down the geography of the metropolitan area more finely, two of the outer ring counties—DuPage and Lake—actually showed wage effects similar to the inner ring coefficient for the rest of Cook County in the equation above. More critically, when the place-of-work effects are broken down by educational level, with interaction terms, their size increases with educational level. The outer suburbs are a relatively cheaper source for college-educated women than for those who failed to complete high school. Thus the major difference between city and outer suburb wages occurs not among low-skilled males, as sometimes suggested, but among high-skilled females.

The wage equations make it possible to estimate the wage savings achievable by placing the electrical equipment plant in the outer suburbs as compared to the central city.[38] Given average central city wage levels for men and women in manufacturing, the payroll of the thousand-worker plant in the city would be about $32.6 million per year. The same plant in a greenfield location with a comparable workforce would have a payroll of $31.3 million per year—a net annual gain to the firm of about $1.3 million. This private gain from an outer suburban site undoubtedly acts as a major incentive, pulling the plant toward the periphery.

In turn, siting the plant on a greenfield will mean that more of the secondary jobs will also be added in the suburbs, where wages are lower. The resulting wage savings from these secondary workers must also be counted as private benefits. Secondary wages total about $45 million annually. Disaggregating this secondary payroll by nine industries, three locations, and two genders, we can make an estimate of the difference in secondary wages under an outer suburban siting and a central city siting of the primary plant. We find that secondary wages will come to about $770,000 less if the initial plant is placed in a greenfield as opposed to central city site. Not all of this $770,000, however, can be viewed as a net benefit associated with the new siting. To the extent that this wage savings is passed along to consumers, it enters into the general cost of living in suburban areas. If the same workers work for lower wages and then turn around and face lower consumer prices, there really has been no net welfare effect at all.

But to what proportion of the multiplier effect does this observation apply? Clearly, in the highly competitive retail sector, wage savings are likely to be turned into lower prices. In addition, those personal service activities that deal most directly with customers can also be expected to pass savings along. For the Chicago metropolitan area, we estimate that this group of services amounts to about 37.5% of the total of all services. These premises imply that about $200,000 of the $770,000 is in fact passed back to workers as consumers, and hence represents no net benefit. This leaves $570,000 to be included in the basic calculation.

Adding $570,000 in secondary wage savings benefits to the $1.3 million in wage savings in the plant itself yields a total wage savings benefit of $1.9 million. In interpreting this figure, one should keep in mind two points. First, the figure suggests an estimate (presumably a lower bound one) of what mobile suburban workers are willing to give up to take suburban jobs rather than central city jobs. Most of the difference relates to relatively skilled workers who participate in reasonably efficient labor markets. Hence we can conclude that their foregoing of high city wages indicates that they receive at least equal benefits from their chosen workplace. Second, we are implicitly assuming that the employers who hire these workers fully make use of their skills. In particular, this means that employers are not simply using those skills as an unnecessary and uneconomic screening device. To the extent that employers are engaging in such inefficient behavior, the social benefits here attributed to low wages would be overstated.

Land Costs

Outer suburban land is considerably cheaper than land in the central city. This difference provides a second major cost savings to businesses that take a peripheral location in preference to one in the city proper. Prime outer suburban land on the edge of the Chicago urbanized area sold for about $2 per square foot, or $76,000 per acre, in 1995. City land was considerably more expensive, except in the most decayed neighborhoods. Good land for most purposes could be obtained for $5 per square foot, or $218,000 per acre. Land in the inner suburbs sold for an intermediate price, which we take as $3.50 per square foot, or $152,000 per acre.[39]

Recall from the discussion of open space absorption our estimates of land use per worker. Using these estimates and the prices given above we can calculate the total land costs for both scenarios. As in the case of wage differentials this figure is adjusted for the portion of activity devoted to local retail and services, since, under competitive conditions, land cost savings in these industries are passed on to consumers, as noted in our discussion of resident costs and benefits.[40]

The result of these calculations is an estimated land cost saving of about $615,000 from the outer suburban plant siting. We should note that in practice a considerable portion of this difference, indeed almost all of it for a prime plant, would be neutralized by city government land subsidies. We consider the wisdom of such policies and related measures in chapter 5. For the present, we carry out our analysis as if no subsidies were forthcoming.

Business Taxes

In section 2.3, we calculated the local revenue that could be expected from businesses under each case. But assuming that differences in business taxes do not represent different levels of public services, these benefits to the public sector must now be viewed as a cost to the businesses in question. Thus the tax savings achieved under the outer suburban scenario are now counted as a private benefit—a net sum of $550,000 per year.

As we did for wage and land savings, we adjusted this amount for the portion in retailing and services that is passed along to local consumers. Of the total employment that on net "moves" to the suburbs under the greenfield scenario, about 10% is involved in retail and personal services. This leaves an overall gain to businesses of approximately $500,000.

Again, it should be noted that a considerable share of this business tax differential may be offset by city government tax breaks to newly locating or retained firms. Such policy questions are discussed in chapter 5.

Construction Costs

By almost all accounts, construction costs are lower in the suburbs than in the central city; informal estimates place the figure at 10% to 15% less. If we assume that roughly $30,000 per employee would be required in construction costs in the city, then our manufacturing plant and associated business developments under the outer suburban scenario would cost about $5 million less. As for wage and land costs, this estimate excludes savings that are passed on to local consumers. At 5% per year, we estimate an annual savings of about $280,000.

The largest part of the difference in construction costs is due to differences in wages in the central city versus the suburbs; thus the gain to the businesses involved is offset by losses to the workers. As such, this amounts to a transfer that nets out in the calculations. Since no net difference in resource use results, this transfer has no effect on overall efficiency. For this reason, we have not added these estimates into the calculation of net benefits and costs, but will include them when distributional issues are addressed in the following chapter.[41]

The Private Benefits of Employment Deconcentration

Overall, the private benefits of locating the electrical equipment plant in the outer suburbs rather than in the city amount to about $2.6 million per year (see table 2-10). By far the largest component of these benefits comes from the lower wages, and especially the lower wages for women, paid in the outer suburbs. These gains are largely translated into profits for firms with a suburban location, although a portion may be passed along to consumers in the form of reduced prices.

2.6 SUMMING UP

We have now explored all the channels by which plant location influences economic efficiency. Putting together the data on externalities, public subsidies, and private benefits, we find an overall difference between the sites of about $70,000 per year in favor of the central city (see table 2-11). (Note: this figure represents the *difference* between the two

TABLE 2-10.

Annual Private Benefits and Costs of Employment Decentralization

1. Resident benefits and costs	($362)
2. Value of abandonment foregone	(58)
3. Wage differential: gain over city	1902
4. Land cost savings: gain over city	616
5. Business taxes	499
Total private benefits	2597

Note: All figures in thousands of 1995 dollars; ( ) indicates loss.

TABLE 2-11.

Annual Costs and Benefits of Choosing Greenfield Development

1. Externalities	($1,121)
2. Public-Sector Impact	($1,548)
3. Private Benefits	$2,597
Net Benefits or Cost	($ 72)

Note: All figures in thousands of 1995 dollars; ( ) indicates cost. Each entry shows the estimated additional annual benefit or cost ( ) associated with greenfield development of a new electrical equipment plant in comparison to central city development of the same plant. The plant has one thousand workers.

locations. Either location is more beneficial than not having the firm at all.) Given the inherent uncertainties attached to several of the estimates and the total size of the costs and benefits imposed, one should not take this figure too literally. The trail of estimation has been arduous and at points circuitous; throughout, we have had to qualify our argument in numerous ways. We find that greenfield industrial development adds nothing to economic efficiency.[42] Under the circumstances and contrary to much rhetoric on both sides of the issue, the safest conclusion is that the costs and benefits associated with the continuing deconcentration of manufacturing are of the same order of magnitude.

We are relatively certain that continuing manufacturing deconcentration involves no net gain, but perhaps not so sure as to suggest policy on this ground alone. In such a situation policy must pay close attention to distributional considerations as well as to efficiency. Who gains and who loses in greenfield development? With an answer to this question, one can assess whether such redistributions are desirable, indifferent, or unappealing enough to prompt public intervention. Thus, before addressing the logic and value of policies to limit or ameliorate deconcentration, we first turn to disaggregating our various estimates in an effort to determine the distribution of gains and losses.[43]

CHAPTER 3

Distributional Consequences

In the previous chapter we considered the costs and benefits of locating a large manufacturing plant in an outer suburban site rather than a city one. On net such deconcentration neither greatly enhances nor greatly diminishes the nation's real product. But such deconcentration does benefit some while harming others. The purpose of this chapter is to assess the distribution of gains and losses generated by manufacturing deconcentration.

In principle, it is possible to estimate a distribution of consequences across virtually any characteristic of the population. Clearly, however, it makes most sense to focus on characteristics relevant to public policy-making and political action. From this perspective, income and residence seem primary. For present purposes, we continue to divide the population into the same three household income groups ($< \$30,000$; $\$30,000–\$75,000$; and $> \$75,000$) that we used in the efficiency analysis. We divide residence into central city, inner suburbs, outer suburbs, and the rest of the nation. While these two dimensions seem the most significant, clearly others would be worth analyzing as well, such as race, age, and gender.

3.1 THE DISTRIBUTION OF EXTERNALITIES

The value of an externality ultimately depends on the income and tastes of those forced to experience it. Throughout our analysis, we have adhered to the standard assumption of welfare economics that an externality imposes a cost equal to the minimum sum that affected parties would demand to voluntarily accept the externality (or, in the case of a benefit, the maximum sum they would pay to have access to the externality). Following the implications of this assumption, we assign a larger dollar value to an externality if it is experienced by a higher-income person than by a lower-income person. While this may seem unfair to noneconomists, it reflects the fact that higher-income households have the resources and desire to pay more to avoid external costs and to achieve external benefits. Similarly, the relatively well-off also put a higher monetary value on food, clothing, and shelter.

As is standard in cost-benefit analysis, we use such individual valuations to estimate a social total. The reason for doing so is not that harm is somehow intrinsically more upsetting to a rich person than to a poorer one. Rather, the point is that the poor person might have pressing needs that compete with this particular concern. For a relatively small reimbursement, this person might feel he or she is better off accepting the externality.[1]

The following sections take up each of the externalities we discussed previously, and analyze how they are distributed across different income categories and residential locations. As we will see, the lowest income group bears a disproportionate share of the costs of deconcentration, as do city residents more generally.

Congestion

Who bears the burden of additional peak-hour congestion costs? It seems fairly clear that the answer must be current commuters. Those already on the roads suffer the additional time delay generated by new commuters. This population includes all commuters in the metropolitan area, but clearly those with long commutes bear a greater proportion of the cost than those with short commutes. In metropolitan Chicago, middle-income households account for almost 60% of auto commuting hours, while high-income households account for about 25% (figure 3-1).

These numbers might be used directly to distribute total congestion costs. However, economists have argued from both theoretical grounds and empirical evidence that the value placed on commuting time is proportional to income level (Wheaton, 1977). Higher-income workers value an hour more than lower-income workers, about in proportion to their incomes. Given this observation, we have weighted auto commuter hours by household income to obtain a distribution of the value of commuting time spent by each income group. (These data are also presented in figure 3-1.)

Clearly, the major effect of adjusting commuter hours by income is to greatly reduce the share of the congestion externality falling on low-income households and to substantially increase the share falling on high-income households. Since congestion is one of the largest externalities estimated in the previous chapter, these figures imply that middle- and higher-income households bear some significant costs associated with deconcentration.

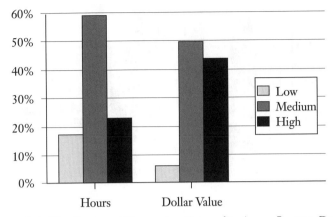

Figure 3-1. Distribution of Congestion Externality Across Income Groups

By residence, commuter hours in automobiles are fairly evenly divided among central city residents, inner suburbanites, and outer suburbanites. As might be expected, the outer suburban commuters account for a disproportionate share of total hours, and central city commuters for a less than proportionate share. Weighting these figures by income reduces the share of central city residents to about 25%, with the remainder divided about equally between inner suburban and outer suburban commuters.

Accidents

Recall that we excluded the costs of accidents to car drivers and passengers, since these are part of the private costs of using automobiles. The externalities consist of those costs borne by pedestrians and bicyclists. Presumably, the incidence of these accidents is roughly proportional to population across income groups (figure 3-2).[2]

But not everyone values an accident at the same dollar amount. Given the large share of total accident costs due to lost work time, it is a reasonable first approximation to assume that individuals value accidents in proportion to their household income. This implies that each income group bears the externality in proportion to its share of regional income (figure 3-2).

By income group, then, about half of this externality falls on middle-income households, 40% on high-income households, and 10% on low-income ones. Tracking the residence of each income group, in turn, suggests the geographic distribution of this externality. By residence, the externality is spread fairly evenly across the city, inner suburbs, and

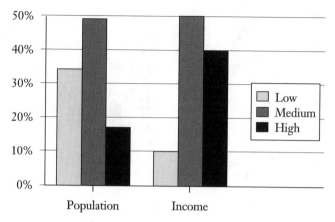

Figure 3-2. Distribution of Population and Income Across Income Groups

outer suburbs. Keep in mind that the overall weight for the accident category is not large.

Pollution

In principle, the incidence of auto-generated pollution externalities is more difficult to determine. Depending on traffic systems, wind patterns, and various other physical conditions, different groups in the region might be exposed to disproportionate shares of this externality. In the absence of detailed information, we assume that exposures are uniform throughout the metropolitan area. However, impacts again should be scaled by individuals' household incomes to reflect differences in their valuing of time. The resulting distributions by both income group and residence follow the same pattern as those for accidents.

Open Space

The key variables determining the externality effects of reductions in open space are population density and per capita income. Again, the distribution of these effects can be expected to vary in proportion to households' income levels, since higher-income households tend to value open space more than low-income households. This leaves the open space externality divided along the same income shares as those used for accidents and pollution.

However, we do not know whether the value of open space varies with households' place of residence as well as incomes. Do suburban families value open space more than central city families? This is a fundamental question with no simple answer; an argument could be made either way. More distant from open spaces, central city families might actually value these spaces more. Alternatively, by moving to the periphery suburban families have demonstrated a preference for access to open space. Lacking any evidence on this question, we simply use the underlying income distribution of the three residential areas to determine the geographic distribution of this externality.

Abandonment

Housing abandonment, by the definition used above, occurs only in developed areas of the central city and inner suburbs. Locating the electrical equipment plant in the outer suburbs rather than in the central city leads to more abandonment. Our estimates suggest that the vast majority (91%) of this increase in the external effects of abandonment will fall on Chicago proper, while only a small share (9%) of the increase will affect the inner suburbs.

In terms of income distribution, clearly all of these externalities take their toll on low-income households residing near abandoned structures. For households that own their homes, the full weight of neighborhood deterioration falls directly on them. Even if they attempt to move out of the area, they must bear the cost in terms of a reduced sale price for their residence.

Unlike owners, renters are mobile, and hence can shift a portion of the externality back on their landlords in the form of lower rents. Poor households are much more likely to rent than middle- and high-income households. For Chicago and its inner suburbs, 64% of low-income households were renters in 1990. Using this figure as an indication of the renter share in neighborhoods experiencing abandonment, we estimate that 36% of abandonment externalities fall on low-income households, 64% on high- and middle-income households. In the absence of any more precise information, we divide this latter figure equally between medium- and high-income households.

Mismatch

The vast bulk of the mismatch externality falls on low-skilled, low-income workers who are denied employment by peripheral plant locations. Such workers are likely to remain involuntarily unemployed or underemployed. Their loss is an efficiency loss to all of society, because their opportunity cost for working is low. That loss is borne largely by themselves.

The only exception to the above is that a portion of the mismatch externality is shifted onto the broad category of all taxpayers. This is because low-skilled, low-income workers and their households become eligible for various transfer programs if they are unemployed. Recall that we have estimated each employed mismatched worker at $12,300 per year. In the absence of employment, what share of this would be forthcoming in transfer payments? Put somewhat differently, what is the transfer replacement rate?

A three-person household collecting AFDC, food stamps, and Medicaid has a cash equivalent income of almost $10,000 (based on Levitan, 1990). But surely not every new mismatched worker will take her or his household into this type of transfer dependency. Many of these workers are young and single; others have working relatives; some will find alternative employment. As a first rough estimate, we assume that 20% of these workers will be in households that increase their use of transfers by $5,000. These estimates imply that 16.3% of the mismatch externality actually falls on taxpayers.

Who pays the taxes to support these transfer payments? While the major transfer programs are financed through the federal government, both politicians and citizens increasingly approach all levels of government taxation as fungible. Thus even though federal taxes are modestly progressive, it seems more defensible to assume that the support of transfer, like tax payments in general, is roughly proportional.

Using this approach, it is still the case that 86% of mismatch costs fall on lower-income households, with about 8% falling to middle-income households and 6% to high-income households. Since mismatch is one of the largest externalities we have identified, these distribution figures imply that low-income households bear a large share of all externalities associated with placing the electrical equipment plant in the outer suburbs.

The geographic distribution of the effects of skill mismatch is somewhat more complex. First, the largest part of the 16% shifted onto taxpayers will be paid by those outside the metropolitan area. For the rest, some parts of the metropolitan area gain from the outer suburban location of the plant, while other parts lose. Locating the plant in the outer suburbs brings substantial benefits to outer suburban low-income workers, but these are not sufficient to offset the losses of central city low-income workers. The estimates suggest that while city residents lose an amount equal to 187% of the total mismatch cost, the outer suburbs gain an amount equal to 115% of those costs. This leaves the inner suburbs bearing a small share of the cost, 12%.

National Externalities

As noted earlier, other parts of the country outside the Chicago metropolitan area will experience externalities as a result of the greenfield development, including congestion, accident costs, pollution costs, and open space costs avoided. Accordingly, we introduce a national category. At the national level the burden of each type of externality is assumed to be distributed across income groups in the same manner as determined for that type of externality in the metropolitan area. But, of course, the weight assigned each type of externality reflects its importance at the national level, not the metropolitan level. Using this approach indicates that 7% of these national externalities are borne by low-income households, 50% by middle-income households, and 43% by high-income households. Since these are gains for the income groups in question, they must be subtracted from other externalities.

Overall Distribution of Externalities

The overall distribution of the externalities generated by greenfield development is just a weighted average of the various categories. Table 3-1 presents a summary by income groups, while table 3-2 presents the corresponding breakdown by geographic areas.

With respect to income groups, about 40% of all the externalities fall on the lowest of our three income groups. This result is largely determined by the mismatch externality, which falls most heavily on the lowest income group. Still, more than half of the externalities come to rest on middle- and high-income households. These are due to their sensitivity to time lost to congestion and other auto-related externalities. Middle- and high-income households are also more sensitive to the open space issue. Thus low-income households are not the only ones to carry the weight of the unpaid costs of manufacturing deconcentration.

Overall, the distribution of external costs by income group is regressive. Low-income households receive only 10% of total household

TABLE 3-1.
Distribution of Externalities by Household Income

	Low	Medium	High
1. Congestion	6%	50%	44%
2–3. Accidents and Pollution	10%	50%	40%
4. Open Space	10%	50%	40%
5. Abandonment	36%	32%	32%
6. Mismatch	86%	8%	6%
7. National	(7%)	(50%)	(43%)
Overall	40%	32%	27%

Note: Subject to rounding error, rows add to 100%. ( ) indicates a benefit.

TABLE 3-2.

Distribution of Externalities by Place of Residence

	City	Inner Suburb	Outer Suburb	Nation
1. Congestion	25%	39%	36%	—
2–3. Accidents and Pollution	29%	37%	34%	—
4. Open Space	29%	37%	34%	—
5. Abandonment	91%	9%	—	—
6. Mismatch	187%	12%	(115%)	16%
7. Rest of Country	—	—	—	(100%)
Overall	96%	29%	(25%)	1%

Note: Subject to rounding error, rows add to 100%. ( ) indicates a benefit.

income, yet they bear 40% of all external costs. Middle- and high-income households receive 50% and 40% of the income shares, respectively. Their shares of external costs are considerably lower.

Table 3-2, showing the distribution of externalities by place of residence, gives a slightly more complicated bottom line. Here we find that the central city bears externality costs amounting to almost 100% of the total. This is possible because the outer suburbs actually gain on the externality account as the result of the plant's location in the periphery. The outer suburbs gain because low-skilled workers from low-income households residing there find employment in the new workplaces. This is the flip side of the mismatch effect. While it is not as large as the losses in the city, it is not insubstantial. The nation as a whole comes out about even, because its share of transfer payments engendered by the mismatch amounts to about the same as the savings it experiences in the form of lower traffic congestion and other auto-related externalities.

3.2 THE DISTRIBUTION OF PUBLIC SUBSIDY COSTS

Next we turn to the second set of costs and benefits, those related to public-sector expenditures. Ultimately, public-sector costs must fall on taxpayers. However, different costs fall on different groups of taxpayers. Given our list of public-sector impacts, the central distinction is between those paid by local taxpayers and those paid by all taxpayers nationally.

Local Fiscal Impact

Our basic methodology calculated the overall fiscal impacts for each scenario from impacts computed by place of work for nonresidential taxes and place of residence for residential taxes. Thus it is relatively easy to disaggregate the local government subsidy geographically.

If the electrical equipment plant chooses an outer suburban rather than a central city location, the central city loses a revenue surplus from nonresidential sources, as well as surpluses generated by more prosperous households. These are funds that are no longer available to the central city and that must be made up by central city taxpayers. The central city actually bears 95% of the overall local impact. The outer suburbs, however, gain a small amount, since under the outer suburban scenario, nonresidential surpluses there outweigh by a small amount the deficits involved in residential expansion. This gain amounts to about 2% of the overall (negative) impact. The inner suburbs are more complex. Under both scenarios, they face a fiscal loss; however, the loss is modestly greater under the outer suburban scenario, amounting to 7% net. The geographical breakdown is clear: while suburban governments gain little if anything from developments occurring at the periphery, the central city loses a great deal.

To determine the distribution of the fiscal impact by income group, we combine the geographic breakdown with information on the income distributions of each type of area. Figure 3-3 shows these distributions. Not surprisingly, Chicago proper, with its higher proportion of low-income households, has a larger proportion of its income accounted for by this group. The city also has a much smaller proportion of its income accounted for by high-income households.

Assuming that local taxes will be raised in a proportional fashion, each area's burden or gain can be distributed among income groups

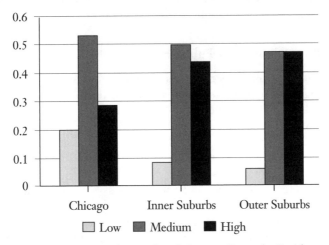

Figure 3-3. Income Shares of Each Income Group by Residence

according to the shares shown in figure 3-3. Aggregating across areas gives the following breakdown for the impact of lost fiscal surpluses (that is, reductions in revenues net of expenditures that must be made up by other local residents): 19% on low-income households, 53% on middle-income households, and 28% on high-income households. The relatively heavy share borne by low-income households is twice their share of metropolitan income. Middle-income households bear about a proportional share, while high-income households bear less than a proportional share. Of course, for both middle- and high-income households, this burden is carried only by households living in the central city.

National Subsidies

At the national level, the implicit income earned on owner-occupied housing remains untaxed. This subsidy, larger under the outer suburban scenario, must be paid for by taxpayers at large. Highway subsidies for outer suburban development are paid for by both state and national taxpayers. Similarly, taxpayers outside the metropolitan area must make up any net fiscal losses in their community resulting from the migration of medium- and high-income households to suburban Chicago in response to development there. Hence from a geographic perspective, these costs do not have to be disaggregated within the region, but simply entered as national costs.

In terms of income distribution, we assume the metropolitan income distribution roughly holds for the nation as a whole. If the taxes used to cover these subsidies will be raised in a proportional basis, then 10% of the costs will fall on low-income households, 50% on middle-income households, and 40% on high-income households.

Overall Distribution of Public-Sector Costs

To estimate the overall distributions of public-sector costs, we follow the same weighted average calculation as for externalities. Table 3-3 shows the distribution by income, table 3-4 the distribution by geography. Relative to income shares, the overall distribution of public-sector costs is mildly regressive; low- and middle-income groups account for about 7% more of these costs than they do of total income. In table 3-4 we see that the public-sector costs of outer suburban development are divided between Chicago residents and the nation as a whole. The suburbs themselves about break even.

This latter observation raises an interesting question: Why do many suburban municipalities aggressively seek manufacturing development,

TABLE 3-3.
Distribution of Public-Sector Costs by Household Income

	Low	*Medium*	*High*
Local costs	19%	53%	28%
State and national	10%	50%	40%
Overall	15%	52%	33%

Note: Subject to rounding error, rows add to 100%.

TABLE 3-4.
Distribution of Public-Sector Costs by Geography

	Chicago	*Inner Suburb*	*Outer Suburb*	*National*
Local	95%	7%	(2%)	0%
National	—	—	—	100%
Overall	57%	4%	(1%)	40%

Note: Subject to rounding error, rows add to 100%. ( ) indicates a benefit.

if the net fiscal impacts of such development are negligible? One possibility is that suburban decision makers lack knowledge concerning likely impacts. Given the considerable energy now devoted to fiscal impact analysis, this explanation seems unlikely. A more convincing explanation of suburban behavior is that individual municipalities put no weight on fiscal costs imposed on their neighbors. When a suburb snags a new plant, it gains the substantial nonresidential surplus generated by that plant. But the fiscal burdens created by associated residential development are spread widely across nearby and distant communities. The lead suburb gains dramatically even if all suburbs as a whole gain little. Like the businesses that focus only on their private profit, these municipalities ignore the broader consequences of their actions.

3.3 THE DISTRIBUTION OF PRIVATE BENEFITS

So far we have analyzed the distribution of the various major costs associated with greenfield industrial development. But just as for our efficiency calculations, we must also consider the various private benefits and costs associated with this decision. How are those gains and losses distributed by income group and geography?

Resident Losses

The largest part of resident losses fall on inner suburbanites who would commute to the city with a city plant, but face lower wages at a greenfield plant. These losses are only partially offset by somewhat shorter commutes for this group. City residents also lose, but relatively few will undertake long reverse commutes to the outer suburbs. (Recall that the welfare losses of those city low-income, low-wage workers who lose employment because of a greenfield location have already been included under the mismatch externality.) On the other hand, outer suburban workers experience modest gains, their reduction in commuting costs outweighing their loss of wages.

Recasting the numbers in terms of income distributions shows more than 60% of resident losses falling on middle-income households, the rest being split about evenly between low- and high-income households. Interestingly, in this case, the distribution of losses by gender shows the bulk falling on women. This result follows from the observation that the outer suburban–city wage differential is much greater for women than for men.

Abandonment

For the private sector, these are losses, or costs of greenfield development. To estimate the distribution of the direct private losses due to abandonment, we simply use the same figures as for the abandonment externality. This means that 91% of the losses are borne by city residents and 9% by inner suburban residents. For the income distribution we take 36% falling on low-income homeowners and 32% each on middle- and high-income households.

Wages, Land Costs, and Business Taxes

The above analysis of wage, land, and tax savings in suburban businesses already discounted these figures for the portion passed on to consumers. The remainder presumably goes into business profits enjoyed by the owners of the various corporations and businesses involved. With respect to income distribution, studies of wealth ownership and capital income suggest that about 75% of capital income goes to the equivalent of our highest income group, 20% to the middle-income group, and only 5% to the low-income group. Presumably the great bulk of these gains would be spread among stockholders and owners across the nation.

The electrical equipment plant considered here is typical of many large oligopolistic industrial firms in the United States. Under these circumstances, any gains from a greenfield location choice accrue to the owners, as suggested above. However, if the primary facility were in a more cost-competitive industry, a portion or perhaps all of the gain would be passed on to customers around the nation. In such a case, the distribution of benefits would be considerably more progressive although still concentrated outside the metropolitan region.

Construction Costs

In our overall efficiency calculations, we made no entry for construction cost differences between the city and suburban areas because this was a pure transfer. Higher costs in the city represented a gain to construction workers but a loss to those investing in new facilities. While such a transfer cancels out in the measurement of efficiency, it does affect income distributions; some groups gain and some lose.

If the plant locates in the outer suburbs, we assume construction workers lose exactly the same amount that the owners of the new business gain. The workers' losses are distributed proportionately across the earnings of all construction occupations. This implies that 10% comes from low-income households, 80% from middle-income households, and 10% from high-income households. The gain then goes to owners of capital, which by income group implies gains of 5% of the construction cost savings to low-income households, 20% to middle-income households, and 75% to high-income households. On net, then, the high-income group gains an amount equal to 65% (or 75% − 10%) of the overall reduction in construction costs. The low-income group loses 5% of that sum and the middle-income group loses about 60% of it.

In terms of geography, the transfer is from construction workers in the Chicago metropolitan area to capital owners nationwide. These construction workers are about equally divided among city, inner suburbs, and outer suburbs. Hence each of these areas loses in wages an amount equal to about a third of the construction cost savings. The gain goes to capital owners who for the most part live outside the region.

The Distribution of Private Benefits

Adding up the various categories of private benefits gives us the distribution by household income shown in table 3-5 and the distribution by geography shown in table 3-6.

In terms of income distribution shares, clearly the major effect of the choice of an outer suburban location takes the form of substantial gains for the highest income group. This is largely the result of their considerable share of the capital income gains achieved through lower wages and taxes.

TABLE 3-5.

Distribution of Private Benefits by Household Income

	Low	Medium	High
1. Resident	(17%)	(62%)	(21%)
2. Abandonment	(36%)	(32%)	(32%)
3–5. Wages, land costs, and taxes	5%	20%	75%
6. Construction	(5%)	(60%)	65%
Overall	2%	7%	90%

Note: Subject to rounding error, rows add to 100%. ( ) indicates a loss.

TABLE 3-6.

Distribution of Private Benefits by Geography

	City	Inner	Outer	National
1. Resident	(48%)	(69%)	18%	0%
2. Abandonment	(91%)	(9%)	0%	0%
3–5. Wages, land costs, and taxes	0%	0%	0%	100%
6. Construction	(33%)	(33%)	(33%)	100%
Overall	(12%)	(13%)	(1%)	127%

Note: Subject to rounding error, rows add to 100%. ( ) indicates a loss.

Geographically, the gains are largely achieved not by Chicago area residents, but by those who live outside the region. These gains take the form of reduced costs for capital owners nationally. This may be a modest overstatement, since some of these capital owners do in fact live within the region. But a small adjustment for this could not significantly affect the overall picture. Within the metropolitan area, the outer suburbs gain a bit, while the city and inner suburbs lose. But these changes are relatively small compared to the overall size of the national gains. It should be noted, however, that had we counted the labor mismatch costs as a private loss to city and inner suburban residents (rather than as an externality) this table would show large negatives in the first two columns.

3.4 THE OVERALL DISTRIBUTION OF GAINS AND LOSSES

We are now in a position to summarize all the gains and losses described in the last three sections. Table 3-7 presents these figures by household income groups, table 3-8 by location. The last line in each table shows the dollar amount for each group.

TABLE 3-7.

Overall Distribution of Costs and Benefits by Household Income Groups

	Low	*Medium*	*High*
1. Externalities	(40%)	(32%)	(27%)
2. Public-sector costs	(15%)	(52%)	(33%)
3. Private gains	2%	7%	90%
Total	($636.)	($970.)	$1534.

Note: Subject to rounding error, each of the first three rows adds to 100%. Last row in thousands of 1995 dollars. ( ) indicates a loss.

TABLE 3-8.

Overall Distribution of Costs and Benefits by Residential Location

	City	*Inner*	*Outer*	*Nation*
1. Externalities	(96%)	(29%)	25%	(1%)
2. Public-sector costs	(57%)	(4%)	1%	(40%)
3. Private gains	(12%)	(13%)	(1%)	127%
Total (in thousands)	($2268)	($733)	$273	$2663

Note: Subject to rounding error, each of the first three rows adds to 100%. Last row in thousands of 1995 dollars. ( ) indicates a loss.

Overall the results of deconcentration are highly uneven. A considerable redistribution is taking place. As table 3-7 shows, more than $1.6 million per year is lost by lower- and middle-income households. High-income households then gain almost the same amount.

Table 3-8 indicates that many of the gainers live outside the region, where they experience the gains in the form of higher private returns on capital investments.

In terms of the normative principles of applied welfare economics, these estimates support the case for public intervention to slow the deconcentration of manufacturing employment. They suggest that such efforts, if effective, would have no major effect on overall efficiency while contributing significantly to the improvement of equity.[3]

Again, however, we postpone our discussion of policy. Since many suggested interventions would affect not only manufacturing, but also service activities, we use the next chapter to repeat our cost-benefit and distributional analyses for the location of a major mixed business service complex.

CHAPTER 4

Business Services Deconcentration

While manufacturing deconcentration has contributed to the growth of the outer suburbs, the spread of rapidly growing service activities has been the hallmark of the new edge cities. While some locally oriented services have simply followed population to the outer suburbs, large-scale producer services and back-office employment have increasingly chosen the outer suburbs as profit-maximizing locations from which to serve regional, national, and international markets.

Any number of outer suburban municipalities are eagerly seeking such development in preference to an expansion of manufacturing. The service activities filling the new office complexes on the metropolitan periphery differ dramatically from nearby manufacturing plants. They draw on a different, more female, labor force; have much lower space requirements; and do not directly pollute. Given these considerations, a cost-benefit accounting of the ongoing deconcentration of these new services might yield different conclusions than those we made for manufacturing. This chapter presents such an analysis.

As for manufacturing, we consider two alternative locations for a prototype facility. One is a greenfield site, and the other is Chicago proper. The facility is a mixed business services office building. To maintain comparability, we set the total business service labor force at one thousand workers. Taking the same approach as for manufacturing, we ask what difference it makes if this mixed business services complex picks a greenfield location in the outer suburbs, rather than taking a site in the central city.

4.1 JOBS AND PEOPLE

Much more than manufacturing, the service sector draws on nonprimary workers who are supplementing their households' income. These workers are more likely to pick their job locations with respect to their residential location, not vice versa. With their low wages and limited commodity purchases, business services also create much smaller multiplier effects than manufacturing. Together these characteristics generate a set of demographics for the business services workforce that is quite different from that generated by manufacturing. This is true regardless of site location.

As before, we continue to conceptualize the basic demographics of the labor force in terms of workers' residential locations, household incomes, and gender. For present purposes, the key difference between manufacturing and the services originates in the heavy reliance of services on women workers. About 35% of manufacturing workers, regardless of plant location, are women; but fully 56% of service workers in the city and 62% of those in the outer suburbs are women.

As indicated earlier, women workers on average take shorter commutes than men. Thus it is not surprising that for both initial sites, the residential distribution of service workers is highly concentrated (see figure 4-1). As a result, a service facility can be expected to generate fewer automobile commuting miles than the manufacturing plant, regardless of initial siting. This observation is further strengthened by the fact that women are less likely to commute by car than men.

In part, because of their reliance on women workers, services show a more unequal distribution of income than manufacturing does (compare figures 4-2 and 2-2). Both the low-income and high-income groups account for larger shares of income among service workers compared with manufacturing workers. This is true regardless of the location of the service facility.

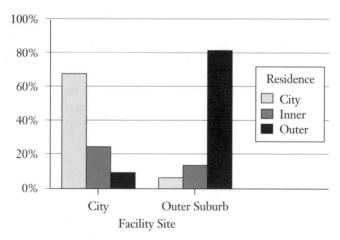

Figure 4-1. Residential Distribution of Service Workers by Facility Site

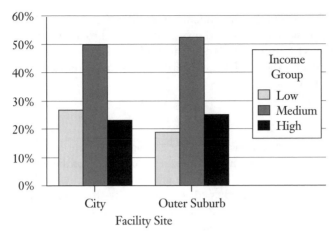

Figure 4-2. Distribution of Service Workers Across Income Groups

As suggested above, a business service facility can be expected to induce less economic activity than a manufacturing plant. To determine just how much less, we again turn to the REMI model for the Chicago metropolitan area. This model suggests that each new business services job generated only about half of an induced job, as compared to a figure of 1.4 for primary jobs in the electrical equipment plant.[1]

In sum, a new business service expansion will produce only modest net additions to the region's population.[2] The smaller multiplier obviously limits population growth. In addition, the greater share of women workers in business services points toward a greater share of supplementary workers in these activities, workers who choose their residence before they choose their workplace. With more supplementary workers drawn from the existing local labor force, relatively fewer new households are drawn to the area by business service growth.

All told, compared with a manufacturing plant, a mixed business service facility is likely to have less population impact. Moreover, that impact is likely to be relatively concentrated geographically. Together, these imply fewer externalities or public costs attributable to the new facility, regardless of location. On the other hand, these facilities can take considerable advantage of the lower wages of suburban women; this fact affords the chance for substantial net positive benefit.

4.2 EXTERNALITIES

A new greenfield business service facility generates more external costs than a similar central city facility. This conclusion holds to a varying degree for each of the component externalities (see table 4-1). The basic theories, methodologies, and qualifications used to derive this table are the same as for the electrical equipment plant. However, a few comments are in order on the two largest externalities—congestion and labor force mismatch.

Congestion

The sizable congestion externality estimated for the business service facility reflects the fact that business service workers in the outer suburbs drive, while those in the city are much more likely to use public transit. This tendency is strengthened in this case by the high proportion of women in the business service labor force. In the city, women are more likely to use public transit than men.

Spatial Mismatch

Siting the business service facility in the outer suburbs leads to the employment of 166 low-wage workers from low-income households. If the same facility is located in the central city, 216 such workers find employment—a difference of 50 in favor of the central city location.

The small proportion of low-wage jobs going to low-income households under a greenfield location again reflects the fact that in the outer suburbs, many of these low-wage jobs are taken by supplementary wage earners in middle- or high-income households. In the city, more of them are taken by primary wage earners of low-income households.

TABLE 4-1.

Annual Externalities Generated by new Business Services Facility Locating in the Outer Suburbs Rather Than Central City

	Outer Suburb–Central City
1. Congestion	398
2. Accidents	42
3. Air pollution	7
4. Open space	39
5. Housing abandonment	20
6. Mismatch	305
7. Rest of nation	91
Total externalities	902

Note: All figures in thousands of 1995 dollars.

4.3 PUBLIC-SECTOR COSTS

Our calculation of public-sector costs builds directly on the base developed for the electrical equipment plant. Again we consider nonresidential surpluses, residential surpluses, homeownership subsidies, and highway subsidies (see table 4-2). The fundamental finding is that the net subsidies for greenfield development of business services are only about half those for the electrical equipment plant. The key explanation throughout is the fact that so many outer suburban service workers are from existing households. As a result, there are fewer new outer suburban households to draw various subsidies.

4.4 PRIVATE BENEFITS

The greenfield business services facility generates considerable private benefits (see table 4-3). By far the largest of these originates in the wage differential between city and suburban labor. In this case, the difference is

TABLE 4-2.
Annual Public-Sector Costs from Business Services Facility
Locating in the Outer Suburbs Rather than Central City

1. Local fiscal subsidy	
A. Nonresidential	185
B. Residential	409
2. Highway subsidy	145
3. Owner-occupied housing	62
4. Rest of country	70
Total cost to public	872

Note: All figures in thousands of 1995 dollars.

TABLE 4-3.
Annual Private Benefits of Employment Decentralization

1. Resident benefits and costs	($333)
2. Value of abandonment foregone	(25)
3. Wage differential: gain over city	1997
4. Land cost differ	206
5. Business taxes	444
Total private benefits	2288

Note: All figures in thousands of 1995 dollars; ( ) indicates loss.

almost $2.3 million annually. The large differential for business services clearly reflects the large wage differentials for women workers, on whom business services rely heavily. The city–outer suburban wage differential is about 10% for women, but only 2.4% for men.

Under the standard theoretical interpretation, this wage differential represents a real efficiency gain to the economy. Presumably, women are willing to work for less in the outer suburbs because they put a high price on their time and a high value on suburban residential locations. These workers would take city employment only at a considerable premium. Business service facilities that locate in the outer suburbs can capitalize on these substantial wage differentials.

4.5 TOTAL COSTS AND BENEFITS

Table 4-4 adds up all three categories of costs and benefits. Gains, driven by strong private benefits, outweigh losses by $515,000 per year. As in the case of the manufacturing plant, considerable uncertainties surround this estimate. Again, the cautious conclusion would be that benefits and costs are of the same order of magnitude, but here with an undertanding that benefits may outweigh costs.

Notice, in this case, that the private-sector gains are substantially concentrated in the initial office facility itself. By far the largest portions of the wage, land, tax, and construction cost gains all accrue to the primary decision makers. Under the circumstances we suspect that the gains of siting the business service facility in the outer suburbs are hardly shared proportionately across either income groups or geographic areas. The externalities and public costs are not likely to be paid by the same people who reap the private benefits. Acknowledging the presence of modest efficiency gains, we must also inquire into the equity of the underlying gains and losses.

TABLE 4-4.

Annual Total Benefits and Costs of Deconcentration of Business Service Employment

1. Externalities	($902)
2. Public-sector costs	(872)
3. Private benefits	2288
Total	515

Note: All figures in thousands of 1995 dollars; ( ) indicates loss. Each entry shows the estimated additional annual benefit or cost ( ) associated with greenfield development of a new business service facility in comparison to central city development of the same facility. The facility has one thousand workers.

4.6 DISTRIBUTION OF COSTS AND BENEFITS

At the finest level of categorizing costs and benefits, almost all of the distributional parameters remain the same as reported in chapter 3. This is because these distributions generally reflect who pays a cost or how a benefit is divided. For example, the siting of the new business service facility has a different impact on congestion than does the manufacturing plant, but the income distribution of the metropolitan commuters who suffer this congestion remains essentially the same for both facilities. The major exceptions to the above proposition are the geographic distribution of the mismatch externality and the geographic distribution of the local fiscal burden. For each of these cost categories, the underlying geography of commuting and new household formation plays a role in determining the distribution of impacts.

Recall that mismatch costs arise from the differential impact of outer suburban and central city locations on unemployed or underemployed workers with few or no alternative opportunities. For the electrical equipment plant, the mismatch costs associated with a greenfield site fall heavily on city residents, although these costs are somewhat offset by gains to low-income workers living in the outer suburbs. For every dollar lost as a result of choosing the outer suburban site rather than the city site, city residents lose about $1.87 that they would have earned under a city plant location, while suburban residents gain the difference (see table 3-2). This geographic distribution of costs is intensified for the business service facility, since compared with the electrical equipment plant, that facility hires a greater proportion of its workforce from its immediate locality. In this case, for every dollar lost on net, city residents lose $2.34, while suburban residents again gain the difference.

More significant are the shifts in the geographic distribution of the local public-sector costs. These also shift toward the central city and away from the outer suburbs. Thus where previously the central city bore $0.95 of every dollar lost in choosing the outer suburban over the city location, now the central city gives up $1.22 for every net dollar lost, with the suburbs actually registering an increase. All of this gain comes to the outer suburbs. As noted before, much of the greenfield business service facility labor force is recruited from existing households, and relatively few new households actually move to these suburbs under this scenario. Thus the increases in nonresidential tax revenues are not as severely offset by residential losses, leaving a significant net outer suburban gain.

Tables 4-5 and 4-6 present the summary information on both the income and geographic distributions. These should be compared to tables 3-7 and 3-8. With respect to the income distribution of gains and losses, the estimates suggest that the high-income group benefits strongly from the deconcentration of employment. Indeed, despite the smaller absolute size of the business services scenarios, higher-income households gain almost as much here as in the electrical equipment case. This follows from their high shares for the private benefits derived from wage, land, tax, and construction cost differentials. They also benefit, here, from a lower public-sector share.

The geographic distributions tell a similar story. City residents suffer about $1.8 million in losses annually from the siting of the office complex in the outer suburbs. Residents of the outer suburbs gain about $400,000 annually, largely reflecting the greater employment opportunities for low-income outer suburban residents. The big gainer geographically is the rest of the nation, which takes large private benefits in the form of higher profits for the corporations involved.

Overall, our evaluation of the outer suburban siting of the business services facility is more complicated than that for the electrical equipment firm. Here there is some evidence of an efficiency gain, but as in the electrical equipment case an outer suburban location imposes substantial losses to low-income and Chicago households. The great

TABLE 4-5.

Overall Distribution of Costs and Benefits by Household Income Groups

	Low	Medium	High
1. Externalities	(34%)	(35%)	(30%)
2. Public-sector costs	(18%)	(53%)	(28%)
3. Private gains	3%	9%	89%
Total	($411)	($582)	$1512

Note: Subject to rounding error, each of the first three rows adds to 100%. Last row in thousands of 1995 dollars. ( ) indicates a loss.

TABLE 4-6.

Overall Distribution of Costs and Benefits by Residential Location

	City	Inner	Outer	Nation
1. Externalities	(95%)	(25%)	36%	(16%)
2. Public-sector costs	(83%)	(5%)	20%	(32%)
3. Private gains	(9%)	(12%)	(3%)	125%
Total	($1799)	($557)	$428	$2445

Note: Subject to rounding error, each of the first three rows adds to 100%. Last row in thousands of 1995 dollars. ( ) indicates a loss.

bulk of the gains accrue to those outside the region, although low-income households in the outer suburbs also benefit. Under the circumstances, and given the modest magnitude of the net gain, an effort to soften the burden of deconcentration on those least able to bear it would still seem appropriate. However, achieving such a redistribution is not an easy task. We turn to these broader policy issues in the next chapter.

CHAPTER 5

Dealing with Metropolitan Deconcentration

Some have suggested that interfering with the processes of metropolitan deconcentration invites costly inefficiencies. Yet, as we have shown, the deconcentration of employment farther and farther into the outer suburbs imposes social costs of about the same magnitude as the private benefits it generates. Moreover, these benefits and costs are distributed with huge inequities. The decay that increasingly characterizes central city neighborhoods and inner suburbs has long-run consequences that threaten the viability of entire metropolitan areas. Even in urban areas in the West and Southwest of the United States, which are generally not deconcentrating, but simply adding new growth at their suburban edges, there is growing concern with the problems this poses in regard to traffic, infrastructure provision, and loss of open land.

In the absence of strong new evidence supporting the efficiency of deconcentration, we believe policy should aim to slow down this process and reduce the disparities among parts of the metropolitan area that it leaves in its wake. So many political, economic, social, and fiscal structures contribute to deconcentration, it is impossible to discuss all the policies that either promote or mitigate it. For instance, changing the tax exemption for home mortgage interest, increasing gasoline taxes, or changing the rules governing depreciation of new real estate investment all would have effects on the relative attractiveness of new suburban development. Some of these, such as eliminating or reducing the home mortgage tax exemption, are unlikely to be changed significantly within the foreseeable future. Others, such as raising the gas tax, might happen for reasons entirely unrelated to metropolitan deconcentration.

A wide variety of policies are now being proposed or implemented with the aim of reducing the pace of suburban expansion or the inequities in the distribution of its benefits and costs. These range from efforts to make the central city more attractive to investors to imposing limits on suburban growth. Some aim to constrain growth or to allocate the costs more accurately to those who cause them; others aim to redistribute the benefits of growth more equitably. A third group seeks to enhance the efficiency of places that are presently less efficient in market terms.

This chapter reviews the main policy approaches within these three groups. For each approach, we begin with a brief description of its history. We then survey the research on the policy to date. Finally, we present our views on how the policy might be used or adapted to slow deconcentration in the future. These suggestions are advanced primarily with reference to cities and regions in which deconcentration is taking place. However, many of the policies discussed here have been advocated by their proponents more broadly as cures for suburban sprawl. Much of our discussion remains relevant to this broader debate, but the reader should note that outside the realm of deconcentrating cities we can claim no special insight into the ultimate costs and benefits of decentralization. The policy approaches include:

Policies that constrain deconcentration or allocate costs more equitably
1. Instituting congestion pricing
2. Imposing impact fees
3. Developing growth management

Policies that redistribute the benefits of deconcentration and growth
4. Encouraging reverse commuting
5. Creating affordable suburban housing
6. Promoting tax-base sharing
7. Expanding special service or taxing districts

Policies that enhance competitiveness
8. Attracting growth back to older areas
9. Establishing regional governance

It is clear that a plethora of tools exists with which to address the problems identified in the previous chapters. The specific mix of policies that is most likely to be both feasible and successful will vary by area. In many cases, the research on factors contributing to success is limited. In general, however, the most promising response seems to be to impose impact fees and some form of growth management to reduce growth in the outer suburbs, while simultaneously establishing programs to increase the attractiveness of investment in the central city. Some of the other policies, such as reverse commuting, suburban affordable housing programs, and special service and tax districts are desirable and feasible at a small scale but appear unlikely to have major effects.

Tax-base sharing and regional governance are not very viable politically and thus are unlikely to be widely adopted. Because all policies are limited in either political feasibility or effectiveness, it is important to pursue a multipronged approach. Furthermore, we continue to need more research on the unintended consequences of policies and programs not explicitly aimed at metropolitan deconcentration.

5.1 POLICIES THAT CONSTRAIN DECONCENTRATION OR BETTER ALLOCATE COSTS

Instituting Congestion Pricing

One of the largest social costs of employment deconcentration is the traffic congestion caused by commuters. It seems reasonable to have a mechanism that accounts for these costs and imposes them on the people who cause them. The most efficient of these methods is peak-hour road pricing, also called congestion pricing, in which motorists are charged higher tolls on congested highways during peak hours.

Proponents argue that congestion pricing "is the only urban transportation policy with a chance of substantially reducing congestion at the busiest times" (Small et al., 1989, p. 98). Presumably, once commuters weigh their options and choose other routes, the traffic on the highways will return to the economically optimal level. Estimates of the value of time savings and reduced accidents range from $20 million to $60 million annually for a large city. Additional benefits would accrue if congestion pricing on highly traveled roadways stimulated mass transit ridership or car pooling (ibid.).

Small et al. (1989) summarize some of the standard objections to congestion pricing as follows. Unlike utility costs, highways traditionally have been publicly funded. Congestion pricing represents a government charge for travel, which has traditionally been considered a fundamental right of motorists. Indeed, constituents may view congestion pricing as a tax increase. Also, bond financing of existing roads may not allow the introduction of pricing mechanisms to reduce traffic during peak hours. In addition, congestion pricing may be opposed because the traditional way of alleviating congestion is by building new roadways or improving old ones. Finally, to be effective, peak-hour pricing must be relatively steep, making its adoption problematic. In sum, critics contend that congestion pricing is inequitable, politically unfeasible, inefficient, and an invasion of privacy. As Small et al. put it, "[s]eldom has applied economics produced an idea with such unanimous conviction in both its validity and political unacceptability" (1989, p. 86).

Opponents also argue that congestion pricing is a regressive fee that is more likely to induce lower-income drivers to change their habits than higher-income drivers. However, the regressivity depends on how the revenues are used. Revenues generated through congestion pricing can be channeled toward reducing fuel, sales, or property taxes, or toward lowering automobile registration fees. Small (1983) argues that these benefits have a positive impact on the general population as well as on low-income motorists. Downs (1992) notes that the public will probably oppose such a program if the revenues are directed to general government expenditures rather than to transportation improvements. Downs also maintains that the success of a congestion pricing program that redistributed funds to lower-income households would partly depend on how extensive it was.

The most efficient method of peak-hour pricing is to have automobiles be identified by cameras or electronic sensors. Some find this an invasion of privacy, but there are ways to preserve the privacy of motorists and still register fees electronically. Many states now use some type of electronic credit cards.

Congestion pricing has had limited application worldwide. Bergen, Oslo, Singapore, and Trondheim have instituted peak-hour pricing in specific downtown zones. Singapore's program appears to have been quite successful both economically and politically (Small et al., 1989), but Hong Kong discarded a more extensive effort less than a year after it was tested. While congestion pricing has never been attempted on a comprehensive level in a metropolitan area, the idea continues to be studied. The 1991 Intermodal Surface Transportation Efficiency Act mandates a Congestion Pricing Pilot Program of five demonstration projects in the United States, and modest alternatives are also being proposed, such as imposing congestion pricing on only small parts of the roadway system (Liu, 1995).

Depending on local conditions, congestion pricing could have a variety of effects on employment deconcentration and residential sprawl. If a complete system of congestion pricing were instituted, it would raise revenues equal to the congestion costs we estimated in the previous section. In tight labor markets, firms would have to reimburse employees for the congestion fees they pay, either directly or through higher wages. This would make it more attractive for firms to choose locations that are accessible without causing additional congestion. On the other hand, when the labor supply is ample, workers would have to bear the costs themselves and would have an incentive to seek work closer to home. Firms and workers might also respond not by relocating but by developing more flexible work schedules. On the whole, the direct effect on deconcentration is likely to be quite small. Nonetheless, reducing congestion would certainly reduce the costs of employment deconcentration.

Imposing Impact Fees

Impact fees are charges that localities impose on developers to generate revenue, instead of making existing residents pay for the new or improved capital projects that development necessitates. Impact fees can cover the costs of schools, roads, or other public infrastructure. At present, individual municipalities are the main governmental units that impose impact fees. Since the costs that new business development generates often spill over into other municipalities, it would make sense also to consider regional or statewide impact fees, for both residential and business development.

Impact fees are assessed for a growing range of purposes, including utilities, roads, waste water treatment facilities, hospitals, schools, public cemeteries, solid waste facilities, and administration buildings, as well as items such as loss of biodiversity, loss of farmland, or the provision of public art. The range of assessed fees varies throughout the country, depending upon the facility and jurisdiction (Angell and Shorter, 1988; Ashworth, 1996; Nelson et al., 1990).

Impact fees are usually imposed according to a formula, and intended to fund infrastructure or services for the new development or for a proportionate share of existing infrastructure and services. Related mechanisms include contributions by developers to public purposes negotiated on a case-by-case basis; exactions, which refer to private provision of infrastructure; special assessment districts, which levy a separate tax on owners for a special purpose; or user charges (Levine, 1994, p. 210).

It is impossible to do a precise accounting of impact fees because they are labeled with a broad range of terms. Nonetheless, it is clear that they are widely used. As early as 1985, communities in thirty-six states assessed some form of sewer impact fees, led by California, Florida, Washington, Oregon, Colorado, and Texas (Frank et al., 1985). Since that time, the practice has spread rapidly. Early studies indicated that impact fees were best applied in high-growth areas because of the danger they pose of slowing development in low-growth areas (Johnson, 1990). However, even in low- or negative-growth states, such as New York and Pennsylvania, impact fees are not uncommon. Altshuler and Gomez-Ibanez state that "[r]arely has a practice spread so quickly at the grass-roots level as land development exactions" (1994, p. 65).

Impact fees are desirable tools for local governments because they are politically palatable to voters. They allow new growth to take place without requiring current residents to pay the costs associated with new residents or businesses; thus they serve both pro-growth and anti-tax sentiments. At the same time, slow-growth advocates like impact fees because they may reduce the rate of growth, especially if surrounding communities do not adopt them. Since impact fees may be used either to expand public services and new development or to upgrade existing public facilities, they are a popular method by which localities can raise revenue during times of declining federal and state assistance for local government. Even developers may support a system of impact fees because it introduces rationality and predictability into what otherwise might be an ad hoc process of negotiations. Furthermore, imposition of the fees requires careful analysis and infrastructure planning by the municipality, increasing the likelihood that adequate public facilities will in fact become available (Nelson et al., 1992; Johnson, 1990). Impact fee programs are most successful when they are one element in a formal plan developed through an open planning process (Angell and Shorter, 1988; Porter, 1988).

Impact fees have been criticized for a number of reasons. Initial challenges focused on their legality. These have largely been resolved, with the courts holding that local governments have the authority to levy charges but have to meet the "rational nexus" test, establishing the connection between the fees and actual, proportional costs imposed by a new development (Ross and Thorpe, 1992; Stroud, 1988). However, several other questions about impact fees remain unresolved: who really bears the burden of impact fees, whether they shift the spotlight away from more important land use questions, how to calculate the level of fees, and what effect they have on competitiveness.

Who really bears the burden of impact fees?

In the case of residential development, developers pass on the burden of impact fees to new home buyers and renters. While this raises the price for newer households, it also increases the value of existing housing, creating windfall profits for current residents at the expense of the new residents (Altshuler and Gomez-Ibanez, 1994; Singell and Lillydahl, 1990). Residential development impact fees have a further regressive effect on lower-income households because the fees are usually based on the size rather than the value of a dwelling.

The fact that the fees are regressive does not appear to be problematic if one is mainly interested in accounting adequately for the costs of new development. By law, impact fees have to be based on a reasonable calculation of actual costs. If the resulting expense slows down growth in a particular place, it will likely be redirected somewhere else, where greater efficiencies exist. Even the equity argument raised appears specious. When development costs are artificially low, households are able to move to new areas and impose their own negative consequences on those left behind. Assessing fair costs on those who seek to move to new areas does not appear unreasonable, even if in the process some current residents in desirable areas reap windfall profits.

Do impact fees shift attention away from important land use questions?

Some observers fear that impact fees will replace land use controls as the main planning tool. When impact fees are in place, planners focus on whether developers are able to pay, rather than whether the character, location, or size of the proposed development is desirable (Siemon, 1987 in Levine, 1994). Thus, for instance, impact fees may affect the socioeconomic character of a community if developers decide to stop building lower-income housing. Eventually, impact fees may prevent minorities from moving into a community because the fees raise the cost of housing. Indeed, Connerly argues that "[i]nstead of pursuing such historic ideals as advocacy planning or 'the City Beautiful,' those who become 'impact fee planners' enhance the idea of 'the City Selfish,' and narrow the focus of the profession to helping existing residents save money" (1988, p. 77).

Despite the lingering questions about impact fees, they have become widely accepted as a mechanism to recover costs. Whether they can be successfully applied as a growth management tool is still unclear, though. Some commentators believe that well-designed impact fees can be used to encourage certain types of development and exclude unwanted development, as long as the policy is based upon reasonable needs and assessments (Nelson et al., 1990). However, others contend that attempts to use impact fees to manage growth have been unsuccessful in California and Florida; they argue that impact fees should be seen strictly as a fiscal management instrument.

Land use planning should clearly be based on more than just the ability to pay. At the same time, a financial mechanism such as impact fees is often easier to administer and more acceptable politically than direct land use controls. The latter, based on values and political choices, are subject to greater attack than impact fees, which are based on actual cost calculations. In reality, impact fees clearly have an important place in a land use planning system.

How should the levels of fees be calculated?

In particular cases, developers have filed court challenges contesting whether a rational nexus—a logical, direct, and clear connection—exists between the new development and the new demand it creates, on the one hand, and the level of the impact fee and its utilization on the other. Tindale (1991) notes that early transportation impact fees did not draw many legal challenges because the fees were relatively modest in relation to actual cost. He cautions against inadequate impact fee calculation because opposition will increase as communities assess impact fees closer to actual costs in the future. However, as experience has increased over the past decade, there are also far more precedents on which to build an argument regarding specific fees.

How will impact fees affect competitiveness?

The additional cost of the impact fees may make a development project uncompetitive with similar developments in neighboring communities since it is generally accepted in theory that impact fees slow growth by raising the cost of new development. At least in the long term, the adoption of impact fees should reduce the number of new homes built by raising the costs of construction (Singell and Lillydale, 1990).

On the other hand, there is evidence that impact fees have not harmed the competitive position of communities and developers in high-growth areas (Angell and Shorter, 1988) and could in fact encourage development in the municipalities that impose them. For example, by offsetting the costs of new development, impact fees are designed to lower the property tax burden on the rest of the municipality. This lower tax rate could then encourage new residential development by increasing demand for homes there. In addition, because impact fees allow for the construction of infrastructure that would otherwise not be provided, they may increase the value of that land and make development more likely (Skidmore and Peddle, 1998).

Impact fees are also attractive to developers who may otherwise fear surprise exactions late in the development process. Instead, developers prefer to receive a reliable assessment from the beginning. Other researchers note that developers grudgingly accept impact fees because the alternative may be a moratorium on development (Nelson et al., 1990). Finally, when impact fees are in place, there is less chance that a developer's project will be stalled because infrastructure funding is not available from the municipality (Goodchild et al., 1996).

Such issues are difficult to research, since impact fees have been used most widely in high-growth areas, where development is more likely to occur anyway. Furthermore, even the more general research on growth management appears to be open to debate. It is particularly hard to assess the effect of any one particular policy tool. Thus, while estimates could be made of how much revenue would be generated by different levels of impact fees, it is harder to know to what extent the implementation of such fees change the behavior of developers and purchasers.

While research in this area is just beginning, a recent study concludes that imposing impact fees does have a net effect of decreasing residential development. Analyzing a sample of municipalities in DuPage County, Illinois (a high-growth, collar county of Chicago), the authors determined that the presence of fees significantly reduced the rate of new residential development. Whereas the average residential growth rate in

DuPage County from 1977 to 1992 was 4.3%, their models showed that the adoption of impact fees by the average municipality would cause the rate of growth to fall to 3.0%. In other words, residential development would slow by 29%. The authors did find that this slowdown was offset somewhat by the effect of lowered property taxes, but by only about 4%. Therefore, the authors determined that impact fees had a net effect of decreasing the amount of residential development that would otherwise occur by 25% (Skidmore and Peddle, 1998). However, the authors caution that several questions still remain to be answered, including whether developers tend to flee to municipalities that do not have impact fees, thereby increasing the rate of development there.

Considering the costs of development on a regional as well as a local level leads to the possibility of regional impact fees. Particularly in dense suburban areas with many small jurisdictions, additional costs for infrastructure and services are rarely limited to one municipality, especially in commercial or industrial development. Yet there are few instances of such a regional perspective. As early as 1976, the American Law Institute established a Model Land Development Code for managing the impacts of regional development. This model code contained no proposal for systematic impact fees, but it pushed municipalities to look at effects beyond their borders in terms of tax burdens, job provision, and affordable housing (Williams, 1991). While never implemented broadly, it influenced practice in several states, including Colorado, Florida, Georgia, Maine, Massachusetts, Minnesota, and Vermont. The major example is the Florida Developments of Regional Impacts (DRI) approach, which requires that all large projects be reviewed by a regional planning agency and the state's Department of Community Affairs. Local governments retain the responsibility for accommodating issues raised in the review and final approval, if necessary by negotiating with other local governments. Thus impacts and costs beyond the development's municipality are addressed.

In Massachusetts, the Cape Cod Commission has the right to approve all developments beyond a certain fairly modest size. It also has the power to impose conditions to mitigate adverse impacts, conditions such as open space and wetlands preservation, or provision of roads or public transportation. In New Jersey, a similar system is being contemplated that would focus on projects with a clear intermunicipal impact; county governments would be the responsible agencies (Morris, 1997).

On the basis of such experiences, the American Planning Association has published a legislative guidebook recommending that supralocal review of developments with regional impacts be made a component of all land use planning (1997). This regional perspective could be expanded to include a system of impact fees at the county level, especially to capture and offset many of the public costs imposed by new business development. As detailed analyses and economic modeling show the impact of development, a case can be built by which regional impact fees can meet the rational nexus test. Regional fees could both reduce the attractiveness of development on the suburban fringe and provide resources to mitigate the imposed costs.

Developing Growth Management

Growth management is an explicit, ongoing program to shape or control growth through some combination of intervention techniques and policies. To some extent, each of the strategies discussed in this book can be part of a broader growth management approach. The type of growth management of most interest here is that which takes place at the regional or state level rather than locally. A metropolitan growth management program can have a significant impact on the incidence and distribution of costs and benefits of employment deconcentration. In its most elaborated version, such a program places a clear urban growth boundary around the urban area beyond which new growth is not allowed, with specific plans for increased densities and adequate infrastructure within the growth boundary.

The term *growth management* has meant many different things since the 1960s. Usually it has referred to efforts to establish balance in development. Some interpretations of balanced development place greater weight on distribution of industry, population, or social benefits, while others emphasize such aspects as growth limits or the carrying capacity of the natural environment (Kelly, 1993). In practice, communities have utilized growth management programs for a variety of objectives, ranging from directing to preventing growth. Growth management programs are now widespread after withstanding challenges in hundreds of court cases that examined the legality of local governments' entering into new areas of land use regulation.

Growth management programs fall into the following categories:

- constraints on the intensity of development permitted through zoning or limitations on subdivisions;
- design and capacity standards for lots and buildings;
- requiring adequate public facilities or imposing impact fees in order to restrain growth and to shift costs from the public to the development project;
- reductions in the supply of land open for development and/or restrictions on the locations where development is permitted, overall

or per time period, through caps on population growth, square footage or housing units, or annual permits (Deakin, 1989, pp. 5–6).

At present, ten states have explicit legislation enabling growth management: California, Florida, Hawaii, Maine, Maryland, New Jersey, Oregon, Rhode Island, Vermont, and Washington. The most widely used growth management policies include concurrency planning, regional review, urban growth boundaries, and greenbelts. Florida uses concurrency planning, in which public services and infrastructure must be provided at the same time as new development is built. Additionally, as described in the previous section, several states use forms of regional review that allow neighboring communities to participate in the planning process when a new development affects them.

Oregon has the most extensive growth management controls in the country. Legislation passed in 1973 requires that each municipality evaluate its growth needs and draw urban growth boundaries to contain anticipated development. State funding for infrastructure, transit, and other services is then directed within those boundaries. The system requires that state agencies respond to local planning, but it also forces local planning to meet state standards.

Greenbelts have been created here and there in North America. Using a multistakeholder process, the Greater Vancouver Regional District identified regional growth concerns and priorities. Then member localities identified lands to include in a green zone surrounding the metropolitan area and committed themselves to find individual methods for protecting it. Toronto uses a similar system, although incursions into the greenbelt are not uncommon. Marin County, California, has an extensive greenbelt controlling growth areas in the county, as do the cities of Boulder, Seattle, Cincinnati, and Boston.

Variants on the establishment of greenbelts are programs to preserve farmlands or environmentally sensitive areas within or adjacent to metropolitan areas. The 1996 federal farm bill allocated $35 million over 6 years to assist state and local programs that pay farmers not to sell to developers. Over the past 20 years, a total of 450,000 acres in 18 states has been preserved through the purchase of development rights. However, urban sprawl consumes as much as a million acres per year. As one example, the town of Pittsford, New York, issued $10 million in bonds to purchase the development rights on 1,200 acres. One of the arguments used was that the cost to taxpayers would only be $67 per year for 20 years, compared to net costs of $200 per taxpayer indefinitely if the land were developed and required public services (Feder, 1997).

San Diego recently approved a new land use plan that reduces the amount of regulation and review of development plans required in part of its area, in exchange for a permanent halt to development in selected environmentally sensitive areas (Ayres, 1997).

Effects of Growth Management Programs

Portland, Oregon, has the largest regional growth management system in the country. According to numerous studies, Portland's system has yielded the following benefits:

- preservation of agricultural and forestry land with improvements in productivity;
- efficient provision of public facilities with associated taxpayer savings;
- efficient allocation of land for various kinds of development;
- reductions in travel times and distances;
- improved housing opportunities without loss in affordability (Nelson and Duncan, 1995; Abbott, Howe, and Adler, 1994).

Recently, however, housing prices in Portland have increased considerably, casting into question the latter item above (Fischel, 1997). Perhaps the urban growth boundary was drawn so far out that it took some time for shortages of available land to develop. In Seattle, where the growth boundary was placed much closer to the built-up area, price increases appear to be taking place more quickly (Lang and Hornburg 1997, p. 4).

Growth management programs for individual municipalities have had only limited regional benefits. Often these programs simply redirected growth to adjacent communities, caused local price increases, or did little to change long-term growth patterns (Kelly, 1993). Observers agree that growth controls enacted in Boulder, Colorado, between 1977 and 1982 did not influence the regional housing market; observers disagree about whether the program increased local housing prices (Cooper, 1986; Danish, 1986). Programmatic incentives appeared to increase significantly the number of moderate-priced housing units in Boulder, but there was no apparent increase in lower-priced housing. In some growth management communities, design standards and community priorities brought to a standstill the production of single-family lower-priced housing. Elsewhere, however, growth management appears to have had no effect on housing affordability.

In sum, growth management policies have had uneven consequences on equity considerations. Policies may or may not be designed to affect distributive consequences for low-income households inside or outside the locality. However, several court rulings have held that growth control measures must go beyond providing benefits to the enacting community and may not unduly affect low-income housing in the regional market.

Arguments for and Against Growth Management

The controversy over growth management follows the lines of similar debates over the proper relationship between government and the market. Advocates maintain that growth controls allow a community to mold its own destiny. They argue that existing residents have the right to reap the benefits of growth, even if it is at the expense of others wishing to live in the community. Without controls, inefficient land development patterns inevitably occur because the preconditions necessary for an efficient market do not exist in urban land markets. In this view, uncontrolled growth itself is inefficient and costly to residents, to local government, and to the environment. Consequently, government intervention is justified to address market failure in urban and regional land development (Nelson and Duncan, 1995).

In positive terms, advocates argue that growth management has the potential to achieve the following results:

1) offset inefficient development patterns; 2) take improved (although imperfect) account of the nature of conflicts among different land uses; 3) inform buyers and sellers of overriding public interest in the environment, and desirable development patterns; 4) achieve development patterns that fulfill public policy as defined by elected representatives at all levels of government; 5) reduce negative externalities which result from interdependencies among land uses; 6) provide the optimal level of public goods; and 7) reduce the costs of providing public services (Nelson, 1994, p. 29).

On the other side, growth management opponents argue that an unregulated urban land market provides the most efficient land allocation and development patterns. Growth management, they insist, produces unanticipated consequences and raises the cost of housing in growth management communities (Gleeson, 1979; Dowall, 1984; Fischel, 1997). Thus, a policy designed to limit suburban sprawl may have no benefits, and perhaps may even involve costs, for low-income city residents. Perhaps this is why central city community organizations and others have paid relatively little attention to growth management, which, if properly implemented, might redirect growth back into the city.

Critics also argue that growth management does not produce the environmental benefits that its advocates claim it will, because it simply deflects development elsewhere, yielding no net gain. Critics further maintain that concurrency planning does not contain sprawl and allows development on environmentally sensitive land. Oregon discovered its urban growth boundary planning contained flaws because low-density development continued to proliferate within those boundaries.

Given the criticisms, it is not surprising that growth management programs have often been attacked and have at times been curtailed. San Diego's growth management system, for instance, has had a seesaw history since it was adopted in the mid-1970s (Calavita, 1997). The system identified three development tiers: an "urbanized area" for infill development; the "planned urbanizing area," where development could take place accompanied by impact fees to provide facilities and infrastructure; and a "future urbanizing area" to be closed to development for at least twenty years. Within ten years, however, development had already begun in this latter tier. This led to protests and a ballot proposition that won handily and effectively stopped growth. During this time, growth in the other tiers became intense, and infrastructure development did not keep pace. Plans for citywide impact fees were never implemented, and a development moratorium was soon breached. As the recession of the early 1990s hit, existing impact fees were cut. In a compromise solution, development in the outer tier was allowed, but only at low densities. As a result, only very high-income housing in inefficient low-density development is occurring. Over a twenty-year time period, then, both advocates and opponents of growth controls have had periods of ascendancy.

Requirements for Successful Growth Management Programs

Growth management programs can directly affect deconcentration if they are implemented on a regional basis, but this has only rarely been the case. Successful programs such as Portland's contain urban development and may reduce land speculation along urban fringes, but will also be subject to frequent political uncertainty.

After examining successful state and regional growth management programs, Nelson and Duncan (1995) identified several elements that must be present for growth management measures to succeed. A consensus must exist in the citizenry that growth management measures are needed. A lead actor is required, usually an executive at the state or local level. From the beginning, the public must be involved in a goal-setting process to establish realistic goals and objectives and to decide on the desired urban form. The public should be involved during all stages of the process, especially implementation. A considerable amount of financial and technical resources should be devoted to the program, and there must be coordination among federal, state, regional, and local governments. A streamlined judicial review process should be created that responds to the needs of all interested parties. Finally, the program must be administered by a professional staff large enough to manage it.

To be successful, a growth management program must contain a range of specific policies and strategies. It must establish specific geographic boundaries to growth and minimum density standards. It should include infill and redevelopment policies, efforts to reduce commuting times, support for affordable housing, and impact fees (Nelson and Duncan, 1995; Kelly, 1993).

Regional planning agencies are needed to implement such a program. For instance, federal transportation legislation (the 1991 Intermodal Surface Transportation Efficiency Act [ISTEA] and its successor, the Transportation Efficiency Act for the 21st Century [TEA21]) mandates metropolitan planning organizations for all metropolitan areas with populations over fifty thousand. Given the importance of transportation in shaping regional growth patterns, and in light of the comprehensive nature of the ISTEA and TEA21 legislation, these organizations could take on a much broader planning role in some regions. Elsewhere, existing regional planning organizations or councils of governments could take on this function (Porter, 1997, p. 242). Thus, there exists the beginning of organizational infrastructure and sufficient programmatic experience to develop serious regionwide growth management programs that can address the issue of deconcentration.

5.2 POLICIES THAT REDISTRIBUTE THE BENEFITS OF GROWTH

Encouraging Reverse Commuting

Reverse commuting programs provide inner city residents with transportation to and from suburban jobs. Unlike efforts to attract growth back to the central city, reverse commuting programs do not directly affect the pattern of employment deconcentration. Rather, they mitigate one of its most severe social costs—the spatial mismatch between the supply of inner city workers and suburban labor demand. Many reverse commuting programs also offer a variety of other supportive services. The majority of reverse commuting initiatives have been undertaken in the Northeast and Midwest because of their density, governmental fragmentation, and concentration of inner city poor (Hughes and Sternberg, 1992, p. 35).

Strategies underlying a reverse commuting program will vary because the barriers impeding regional labor market clearance differ across metropolitan areas. In some places, it may be enough simply to reroute the existing public transit or to create a good regional databank on available jobs and workers. Elsewhere, a new transportation system or new job training programs may be needed (Hughes and Sternberg, 1992).

Federal transportation programs have significantly influenced the development of reverse commuting programs. The Entrepreneurial Services Challenge (ESP) grant created in 1987 by the Federal Transit Administration provided start-up funds to entrepreneurs for alternative transportation systems. Eight of the ESP grants for establishing reverse commuting programs went to community-based groups such as ACCEL Transportation, managed by the LeClaire Court Resident Management Association in Chicago. ISTEA and TEA21 also provided resources to facilitate transportation options for inner city residents. The U.S. Department of Housing and Urban Development started the Bridges to Work program, which provides $17 million in funding over four years for reverse commuting programs serving public housing residents in Baltimore, Chicago, Denver, Milwaukee, and St. Louis.

Chicago provides some typical examples of reverse commuting programs. Like their counterparts in other cities, Chicago's inner city residents face the problem of spatial mismatch. For instance, there are fifty thousand jobs located within two miles of three specific suburban rail stations, but existing rail service is not designed to meet the needs of urban residents commuting to the suburbs. As in many other metropolitan areas, Chicago's bus and rail service does not adequately serve inner city residents for three reasons:

• Many suburban jobs are not within walking distance of transit stops.
• Commuters have to spend a great deal of time transferring between transportation modes.
• The transit system is geared toward morning and evening commuters, and does not meet the needs of the second and third shift workers.

Two Chicago programs provide evidence of both success and failure of programs to address these issues. Each day, a not-for-profit organization called Suburban JobLink transports between four hundred and six hundred workers from Chicago's poorest neighborhoods to jobs, mostly in light manufacturing. Between 1970 and 1993, Suburban JobLink located temporary employment for twenty thousand people and full-time employment for another five thousand. The transportation service is underwritten by Suburban JobLink's employment contracting service. Riders and foundations contribute to transportation costs, but the labor contracting service provides 95% of transportation funding (Hughes and

Sternberg, 1992). Under HUD's Bridges to Work program, Suburban JobLink intends to place an additional one thousand to fifteen hundred workers from Chicago's west side in jobs around O'Hare Airport.

ACCEL was started as a transportation and job support program for public housing residents in LeClaire Courts on Chicago's southwest side. It offered a variety of supportive services, such as employment counseling, job training and placement, child care, and after-school programs. It also transported 125 nursing assistants and service workers from housing projects to suburban jobs every workday. Originally the program was designed to serve just one public housing development, but it soon became clear that it needed a larger market to be viable. When commuters using the service did well on a job and obtained permanent employment, they often made alternative arrangements; thus, ACCEL needed a continuing stream of new riders.

ACCEL received funding from foundations, HUD, the Federal Transportation Administration, and local transportation authorities. It met its ridership and revenue goals during the first two years. Thereafter, however, it did not generate sufficient growth to cover more than about half of its costs with income from riders and employers. Unable to maintain external grant support, the service folded in 1995.

Several lessons emerge from this experience:

- Reverse commuting programs require continuing subsidy.
- Because transportation is only one of the obstacles to employment, other supportive services need to be provided as well.
- As with welfare-to-work programs, participation is worthwhile only if jobs pay sufficiently above welfare levels and include benefits.
- A constant inflow of new participants is necessary (Public Private Transportation Network, n.d.).

Reverse commuting programs offer a range of potential advantages and disadvantages. They provide benefits much more quickly than attempts to attract employers to the central city. City residents who find permanent suburban jobs gain additional disposable income that will be spent in city businesses. Additionally, transit systems benefit from increased ridership. On the other hand, reverse commuting programs make it easier for suburban employers to find workers, and thus these programs encourage more firms to leave the central city. This is why urban neighborhood organizations and city agencies have at times been reluctant to support reverse commuting programs (Chicago Department of Public Works, 1990).

Given the reality of where job growth is taking place in most metropolitan areas (especially those that are deconcentrating) and given the job skills of unemployed city residents, reverse commuting programs appear to be a useful way to increase access to suburban jobs for low-skilled inner city residents who suffer most from spatial mismatch. As much as possible, such programs should be integrated into the normal operations of major public transportation systems, rather than continuing to develop as separate programs. Given the very nature of deconcentration, though, reverse commuting will always be more complicated and hence more expensive than reaching most central city workplaces.

Creating Affordable Suburban Housing

Affordable housing programs are another way of helping city and inner ring suburban residents move to the outer suburbs and gain access to the new centers of job growth. Traditionally, private actions, market forces, and local government policies have hindered lower-income households from locating outside central cities or inner suburbs. Minorities are often denied loans by mortgage lenders and steered by real estate agents into certain areas because of their race. Information barriers and an insufficient supply of affordable housing outside the central city prevent lower-income households from freely participating in the regional housing market. Exclusionary zoning policies adopted by suburban governments often reflect and promote de facto racial and class discrimination. Additionally, higher-cost housing provides lucrative benefits to suburban governments because it produces greater property tax revenue.

Creating more affordable housing in locations close to suburban centers of employment will not change the pattern of employment deconcentration, but it will reduce the associated social costs. Greater proximity to jobs will increase employment opportunities for those who would otherwise be unemployed in the central city, reducing the costs of the spatial mismatch. Proximity obviously also reduces commuting costs. Finally, affordable suburban housing may lower the concentration of poor residents in the central city, reducing the fiscal burden and thus drawing other residents as well as firms back into the city, with the potential of further cutting commuting costs.

Some affordable housing strategies explicitly aim to provide lower-income households with the ability to move away from the central city to take advantage of better employment and housing opportunities. Other programs more generally address the existing supply imbalance in the regional housing market by stimulating the production of lower-cost housing outside the central city.

Housing affordability and regional mobility programs are not limited to one formula but are influenced by local needs and circumstances.

Some impose mandatory requirements, while others rely on voluntary participation by developers and municipalities. The concept of affordability itself is subject to a range of definitions and may require very low or above average income. Some programs work with temporary rental subsidies, while others focus on the construction of housing that will permanently be available to low-income residents. Most programs work through either planning mechanisms, financing programs, or various legal procedures such as inclusionary zoning.

Between 1973 and 1993, affordable housing programs produced about 250,000 housing units in the suburbs, with the majority produced between 1983 and 1993 (Burchell et al., 1994, p. 61). Federal housing programs such as HUD's Section 8 Portability Policy and Housing Assistance Plan stimulated a variety of affordable housing strategies at the state and local levels. The majority of affordable housing and regional mobility programs are located in areas with high housing costs, particularly the East and West Coasts. Some of the most active housing strategies take place in California, Connecticut, Massachusetts, and New Jersey, while some of the most notable local programs are found in Boston, Montgomery County (Maryland), and Orange County (California) (Burchell et al., 1994, p. viii).

Planning Programs

Several states require local jurisdictions to develop housing plans that will meet the needs of all income groups. This requires a projection of the number and type of housing units required, and an analysis of whether sufficient land is available with the right zoning to accommodate this housing. California, Oregon, New Jersey, Florida, Vermont, and Washington have the most developed legislation in this regard. While these states differ in how well their municipalities have complied with the requirement to develop such plans, and in the extent to which those plans have been implemented, in general there seems to have been limited effect. Over the past twenty years, new suburban affordable housing units built as part of local affordable housing plans have met only about 10% of the projected need (Burchell et al., 1994, p. 62). Most states have no enforcement of the plans, and reporting requirements are limited. Thus municipalities may announce the number of units needed at different price levels, but may in fact never check specific development proposals against these goals, nor take initiatives to encourage the needed development. In sum, while local affordable housing plans are useful as statement of needs, their effectiveness is minimal without stringent enforcement.

Financing

During the economic boom of the 1980s, several successful financing mechanisms were developed for the construction of affordable housing in the suburbs. Many of these subsequently fell victim, in whole or in part, to the slower economic growth as well as tighter constraints on government spending in the early 1990s and have not been reinstated. This includes exaction-based models such as linkage fees, whereby developers either pay a fee or agree to develop affordable housing elsewhere in exchange for permission to build in a highly desirable area. This approach is viable only during periods of high demand for high-income housing or commercial development.

More resistant to economic cycles but still subject to the vagaries of government policy are housing certificate programs. While few funds are available for constructing new subsidized housing in the suburbs, the federal government is funding approximately 1.3 million Section 8 vouchers and certificates, which provide a rental subsidy for qualifying low-income families in market-rate housing. Only a small number of these have actually been used by central city residents to move to nonpoor suburban areas (Wright et al., 1997).

One of the main examples of successful use of this program is Chicago's Gautreaux program. This program provides opportunities for a maximum of 7,100 low-income people to receive Section 8 certificates to relocate in areas that are not predominantly African-American. In 1976, the U.S. Supreme Court ruled that this model, which provided housing throughout the Chicago metropolitan area, was justified to remedy years of discrimination in locating public housing. Before and after they locate new housing, participants receive supportive services from the Leadership Council for Metropolitan Open Communities. Since the program's inception in 1976, more than two thousand African-American low-income families have found housing in white middle-class suburbs (Rosenbaum, 1993). Similar court-ordered programs have been initiated in other cities, including Cincinnati, Dallas, Milwaukee, and Memphis.

Research on Gautreaux participants indicates that low-income households moving to suburban areas receive greater benefits than households relocating within the city (Rosenbaum, 1993). Participants who moved to the suburbs found more employment opportunities, and their children were more likely to attend college or find well-paying jobs, than their counterparts in the city. Research on the Cincinnati program found that wages and employment opportunities increased when participants moved into white communities, regardless of their location (Fischer, 1993). Counseling and supportive services are critical to programmatic success (Rosenbaum, 1993).

HUD's Moving to Opportunity demonstration program reproduces many of the features of the Gautreaux model. Now being tested in Baltimore, Boston, Chicago, Los Angeles, and New York, the program differs from Gautreaux in that it simply relocates residents from low-income areas to higher-income areas and does not base participation on race.

Inclusionary Zoning

Inclusionary zoning is designed to increase the number of affordable housing units in specific new developments. Generally, this involves setting aside a certain number or proportion of units for people with lower incomes and assuring rent or purchase levels are set accordingly. In exchange, developers are allowed to build at higher densities than would normally be allowed. Although no recent comprehensive survey exists, it is estimated that between seventy-five and one hundred localities have some such program in effect, and that approximately fifty thousand units have been built over the past twenty years (Burchell et al., 1994).

Montgomery County, Maryland, has one of the most comprehensive affordable housing strategies in the country. Under its 1972 inclusionary zoning policy, the county—one of the wealthiest in the Washington, D.C. area—requires that in developments with fifty or more units, 15% must be set aside for low- and moderate-income households. In return, developers may build 22% more units than would otherwise be permitted. Montgomery County's Housing Opportunity Commission can purchase up to 40% of the set-aside units as "deep subsidy" rental units. It also provides financing for buyers and purchases scattered site units for public housing and the elderly. By 1994, 8,842 moderate- and low-income housing units had been created through the county's housing policy. These programs are particularly significant because they spread low- and moderate-income housing throughout the county (Metropolitan Planning Council, 1995).

Other Approval-Process-Based Mechanisms

One other mechanism is an interesting variant on inclusionary zoning. Officially known as "specialized access to appeal or reward," it gives public or private developers the right to sue if local authorities deny permission to build a new proposed development. This imposes significant restrictions on what are considered reasonable grounds for rejecting proposed plans. Unlike local housing plans or inclusionary zoning, this policy does not proactively promote affordable housing, but it removes a significant obstacle—the power of local authorities to engage in excessively restrictive zoning.

This strategy has been primarily used in Massachusetts, and more recently in other New England states. While the purpose of the strategy is the same in each state, each state's program is somewhat different. Specialized access to appeal or reward enables public and sometimes private developers to appeal if local government bodies deny proposals or approve them with conditions negatively affecting their feasibility (Burchell et al., 1994, p. 28). Local authorities may reject plans only if their housing stock already has at least 10% affordable housing units, or if subsidized housing occupies or would occupy too large an area. This strategy has been most effective in Massachusetts, where 12,000 housing units had been built by 1989. The advantage of this approach is that state government does not directly challenge localities, but removes market impediments by facilitating the development process (Burchell et al., 1994, p. 29).

Effect on the Costs and Benefits of Employment Deconcentration

These programs do not have a significant effect on the deconcentration pattern of firms, although they may slightly facilitate it. However, programs such as Gautreaux demonstrate the potential of affordable housing programs to reduce the inefficiency of the spatial labor mismatch in metropolitan areas where employment is deconcentrating. At the societal level, there are significant gains if people now living in the city and not working are able to live in affordable suburban housing and thereby gain access to jobs. There are also savings from the reduction in commuting and its attendant costs of congestion, accidents, and air pollution, if current low-paid workers who live in the city are able to move closer to their suburban place of employment.

Affordable housing strategies are gaining some momentum throughout the country. However, with some exceptions, they appear not to have increased the housing opportunities of their target population, the urban poor (Schill, 1991, p. 847). Instead, suburban low- and moderate-income households have been the major beneficiaries of the increased housing in the outer suburbs (Lamar et al., 1989). Many urban low-income households are ineligible because they cannot meet credit requirements, provide a sufficient down payment, or make their way through a complex process. Thus in the end, these programs may primarily have the effect of lowering housing costs for some suburban residents, further increasing the competitive advantage of suburban locations for firms requiring a diverse labor force. The net effect of suburban affordable housing policies on deconcentration thus remains a question requiring further research.

Promoting Tax-Base Sharing

Tax-base sharing refers to a system whereby taxing bodies such as municipalities share revenue with each other, rather than keeping it all themselves. It is a way of addressing the fact that different cities have unequal amounts of taxable property (both absolutely and per capita) and therefore differ in their ability to raise revenue. This unequal fiscal capacity is both a cause and an effect of employment deconcentration. Municipalities compete with each other for firms because of the fiscal advantages they bring to host communities. This then allows these communities to offer more services or reduce tax rates, further increasing their attractiveness. Tax-base sharing has the potential to reduce competition among communities, while enabling them to offset some of the negative effects of deconcentration.

The most successful case of tax-base sharing has been operating in Minneapolis–St. Paul for the past 25 years under the authority of the Metropolitan Council. Established in 1967, the Council consists of 17 members appointed by the governor. Its area includes 7 counties, comprising 187 local governments and 49 school districts (Mattoon, 1995). Under the tax-base sharing system, each city must contribute to a regional fund 40% of the growth in tax revenue from its commercial and industrial tax base. This money is then redistributed in inverse proportion to the amount of nonresidential assessed property in each municipality. At present, about 20% of the regional tax base is shared through this system, and it has reduced tax-base disparities between municipalities from approximately 50:1 to approximately 12:1 (Orfield, 1997).

Clearly this system reduces but does not eliminate the incentives for tax-base competition. It also creates greater equity in the ability to fund local services (Baker et al., 1991). On the other hand, since the residential tax base is left out of the system, exclusionary zoning is not diminished, and towns with high-valued houses without commercial development disproportionately benefit. Including the residential tax base would further diminish inequities and might reduce the incentive for residents to move out of older communities with stagnant tax bases to newer ones. Since there is limited experience with this model, it is unclear how great its effect on such decisions might be.

How politically viable this model would be elsewhere is another open question. More limited systems exist in Kentucky, where the city of Louisville and the surrounding Jefferson County have an income tax sharing agreement; Dayton and Montgomery County, which share the increased property and sales tax revenue generated by economic development efforts; and Rochester and Monroe County, New York, which have a sales-tax-sharing plan (Parzen, 1997). Even in Minnesota, the system has not been uncontroversial, and its maintenance has required the development of very active political coalitions (Cisneros, 1995). A recent attempt to expand the system by including high-end residential development passed the legislature but was vetoed by the governor (Orfield, 1997). Some have argued that the system managed to be passed in the 1970s only because the Twin Cities then had a homogeneous population, and that it would never pass now (Martin, 1995). Orfield, a researcher and Minnesota state legislator, argues that in most metropolitan areas between 60% and 85% of the population lives in municipalities that would benefit from tax-base sharing. This fact, Orfield claims, creates the potential for a strong coalition almost everywhere. Efforts are now under way in Chicago and Philadelphia to explore the viability of the approach.

Creating coalitions for this and other examples of regionalism is obviously fraught with problems of politics, class, and race. Legislators representing inner ring suburbs may not want to align with central city legislators, even if they share many economic interests, for reasons of race as well as political tradition and alignment. Similarly, African-American and Hispanic legislators from the central city have typically been suspicious of any regional approaches, seeing them as attempts to dilute the strength and control of communities of color. For instance, when Harold Washington, an African-American, was mayor of Chicago from 1983 to 1987, Republicans in the state legislature made several attempts to place major city entities such as the airport under regional control (Clavel and Wiewel, 1991). Coalitions between central city and nonmetropolitan areas of the state may often be more feasible, as they align people against the interests of suburban legislators. However, such a coalition is likely to promote statewide approaches, such as a shift of school funding from the local property tax to statewide sales or income tax, rather than regional approaches.

Expanding Special Service and Taxing Districts

Recognizing the advantages of regional approaches, many suburbs and central cities now cooperate in a large number of special districts or authorities with limited functions, such as transportation or water provision. Such arrangements retain autonomy for local governments, while garnering at least some of the benefits of regionalism. While much more modest than tax-base sharing, special districts probably offer the best hope for increased regionalism in the near future.

Perhaps the major example of a special authority with extensive powers is Metro, the Portland Metropolitan Services District, first established in 1970. With a home rule charter, a directly elected twelve-member board, and local taxing powers, Metro may be assigned such specific service responsibilities as voters or legislators decide. At present, its main responsibilities are metropolitan land use planning and growth management. In addition, Metro runs the metropolitan solid waste disposal system, a zoo, and convention and arts centers (Cisneros, 1995; Metropolitan Planning Council, 1995). The gradual expansion of Metro's responsibilities indicates it is held in high regard.

A particularly interesting type of special authority is that established to fund major cultural and civic facilities such as museums and zoos. Often these institutions are funded by the central city and located there, but are heavily used by suburbanites. In 1988, Denver created the Scientific and Cultural Facilities District to support such institutions as the Denver Zoo, the Denver Botanic Gardens, and several museums. The District is funded by a 0.1% sales tax in the six-county metropolitan area. The Allegheny County Regional Asset District, established in 1993, has a similar purpose and is funded by a 1% sales tax. Half of the revenue goes to museums, libraries, parks, the zoo, and the Three Rivers Stadium; the other half is used to reduce fiscal disparities and to decrease reliance on the property tax.

More common special authorities provide water, sewage treatment, or regional transportation. A major issue surrounding these authorities is that of political control, particularly whether governing members should be elected or appointed, and how many representatives different jurisdictions should have. In Chicago, the Regional Transportation Authority (RTA) is the overarching body that runs the Chicago Transit Authority as well as the suburban bus and rail systems. The RTA is characterized by frequent struggles over the resources allocated to each of the operating systems and has been subject to several reorganizations. Recently, a coalition of community-based organizations launched a concerted campaign to make all of the transportation planning in the region more accountable to the needs of low-income Chicago communities. In particular, the coalition analyzed the composition of the various planning bodies; it argued that they underrepresent City of Chicago government, city residents, transit users, and city transit providers, and that they probably violate federal law (Siegel and Mason, 1995). Questions have also been raised about the cost-effectiveness of special authorities compared to general purpose governments, and their overall effect on regional competitiveness (Foster, 1997).

As special authorities proliferate, they will most likely increase the range of issues subject to some form of regional decision making. At the same time they will increase the problem of democratic control over government functions and may increase the sense of fragmentation as specialized functions are handled by separate bodies. Nevertheless, special authorities are valuable mechanisms that allow for a range of distribution of costs and benefits in different functional areas. Further-more, they create "social capital" for regional collaboration that may make it possible to engage in more regional collaboration in the future.

5.3 POLICIES THAT ENHANCE COMPETITIVENESS

Attracting Growth Back to Older Areas

A key way to reduce the negative effects of deconcentration is to retain and attract residents and businesses back into the central city and inner ring suburbs. Such place-oriented strategies have been a goal of federal, local, and community-based programs for at least thirty years. Federal initiatives such as Model Cities, the Office of Economic Opportunity, the Community Development Block Grant program, and Urban Development Action Grants have aimed at creating more favorable conditions in central city neighborhoods. The most recent version is the Empowerment Zone and Enterprising Communities program, which provides tax incentives for businesses to locate in designated neighborhoods (including inner ring suburbs) and to hire residents from the area; the program also provides direct grants for a broad array of supportive social services.

Municipalities have developed their own programs, some of them building on federal initiatives. Boston, Baltimore, Cleveland, Pittsburgh, and other cities have pursued well-publicized downtown-oriented and neighborhood-oriented approaches. New York City has had a very active and successful redevelopment program for low- and moderate-income housing, Los Angeles focused rebuilding efforts on the South Central area in a less successful effort, and Chicago has been funding an extensive network of neighborhood-based community development organizations for the past fifteen years. Most other cities, especially in the Northeast and Midwest, have undertaken similar programs.

At the neighborhood level, many small not-for-profit organizations have developed to take advantage of these federal and local programs as well as private-sector support. More than two thousand neighborhood development organizations are actively involved in housing and economic development; even more community-based organizations are providing health, crime prevention, educational, or other social services to improve the local quality of life (National Congress for Community Economic Development, 1989; Vidal, 1992).

These place-based efforts have been subject to criticism for many years. One early strand of critique argued that neighborhood revitalization efforts may increase segregation and isolation by keeping (minority) poor from obtaining opportunities to move out (Kain and Persky, 1969).

More recently, there has been a subtle debate among analysts about the relative role of different factors in keeping people and places poor. William Julius Wilson (1987, 1991, 1997) argues there are two key causes. On the one hand, economic transformation—especially the loss of well-paying manufacturing jobs—has reduced job opportunities for African-American men. Simultaneously, a lessening of residential segregation has allowed the African-American middle class to move out of all-black neighborhoods. As a result, poverty in ghetto neighborhoods has been increasing, which in turn decreases the job-readiness of residents. Massey and Denton (1993) instead emphasize the role of racial segregation in creating poverty neighborhoods. They argue that in a situation of rising black poverty, the existence of racial segregation concentrates poverty, regardless of whether middle-class blacks move out.

In an empirical test of these hypotheses, Jargowsky found that metropolitan-wide forces are far more important in accounting for concentrated poverty than neighborhood-specific factors. The most important factor is the overall income growth and distribution in a region, which explains about three-fourths of the variation in ghetto poverty. Jargowsky further found that in regions where incomes rose more and were distributed more equally among households, fewer people lived in high-poverty neighborhoods (Jargowsky, 1997, p. 170).

Findings such as these have been used to argue against a host of place-based and place-oriented strategies. Additional arguments posit that most of these programs are ineffective and do not improve conditions for low-income residents. For instance, Lemann (1994) argues that community development organizations have not moved residents into jobs, even though they have had some success building new housing. Wolman et al. (1994) analyzed cities widely considered to have revitalized their downtowns; they found that job opportunities for low- and moderate-income residents had not increased.

The shortcomings of these efforts may reflect less their inherent limitations than the fact that they have been poorly funded and are up against strong private incentives working toward deconcentration. Indeed, the federal resources devoted to these programs pale in comparison to the deconcentration effects of other federal programs such as highway construction, deductibility of mortgage interest, and the availability of tax-exempt financing and favorable depreciation rules for new construction (Chernick and Reschovsky, 1994). The litany of other urban woes, from the decline in manufacturing to the increased concentration of the nation's poor, is well known. In the face of these problems, even small successes in neighborhood revitalization may be seen as evidence of the enduring potential of central city neighborhoods. Furthermore, even if the regional opportunity structure is more important than neighborhood-specific factors, many programs to address the opportunity structure may well be delivered efficiently and effectively in a geographically targeted manner.

Our analysis in the previous chapters suggests that at the level of society as a whole, the costs and benefits of deconcentration largely cancel each other out. The reverse is also true. Efforts to reconcentrate employment opportunities in the central city may have some costs, but these are offset by significant societal benefits. Thus, well-designed efforts to attract businesses and households back to cities and inner suburbs are far less expensive than their critics have argued. Even in the short run, such programs not only achieve desirable distributional results, but may also improve efficiency. They may actually increase the size of the pie by utilizing otherwise unproductive labor, land, buildings, and infrastructure.

The most promising of these efforts must focus on rebuilding the infrastructure and educational systems of existing viable older areas in the city and inner suburbs, refitting them for new service employment (Wiewel and Persky, 1994). In general, this means building not in the poorest places first, but in those areas that have not yet fallen into decay. There is some evidence that there needs to be a certain minimum critical mass of middle-income residents to obtain positive results. Once several newcomers on a block start housing improvements, other residents will follow. Also, a critical mass is needed before sufficient additional buying power is present to attract new retail uses (Quercia and Galster, 1997). Therefore, targeting selected neighborhoods is more likely to be effective than spreading improvement efforts over a broad area (Turner, 1997).

In any event, even the strongest proponents of people-based or dispersal-oriented strategies, who believe that individual mobility is more important than attempts at neighborhood revitalization, have to acknowledge that central city neighborhoods will continue to be home for millions of residents. Thus central cities will continue to warrant serious efforts at amelioration and revitalization—not as the only strategy, but as an important component of a broader array of regional strategies.

Establishing Regional Governance

The most drastic way of reducing the disparity between the central city and its outer suburbs is to reduce the distinction between them by joining them in one governmental body. This would eliminate or minimize many of the factors that now drive firms to the suburban edge, as well as provide the resources to address many of the negative consequences of deconcentration. While the United States has had several waves of interest in creating regional governments, they have achieved only limited success. Yet some of these earlier efforts are notable examples. The increased pace of deconcentration over the past ten years, combined with the new emphasis on metropolitan areas as the basic unit of international economic competition, has recently reinvigorated interest in regional solutions. Possible approaches include creating regional governments, expanding the authority of the central city government through annexation, and creating regional authorities with limited functional domains.

The Unigov system in Indianapolis–Marion County, established in the early 1970s, offers a good example of both the strengths and the limitations of regional governance. Unigov combined city and county governments, expanded the boundaries of the city from 82 to 402 square miles, and increased the city's population from 480,000 to 740,000. The mayor is the chief executive, and chairs a 29-member City-County Council. Six departments took over from 16 independent special purpose corporations in providing the region with general administration, development, parks and recreation, public safety, public works, transportation, and public health services. Some functions have remained outside the system, as have several municipalities which elected to stay separate (Mattoon, 1995). Notably, education has also remained separate; this is the area in which disparities are most critical and the effect of equalization would be most significant.

The main benefit of the Indianapolis system has been to enhance local fiscal capacity without increasing disparities. A new countywide income tax and other taxes have been instituted, the cost of economic development incentives has been spread over a larger base, and borrowing capacity has increased. However, not all costs of government have been consolidated; especially those associated with public assistance continue to be levied at the township level, borne disproportionately by the 180,000 residents of central Indianapolis (Swindell and Parks, 1995). Furthermore, because of historical development patterns, tax-exempt uses that serve the entire area are concentrated in the central area as well. For these reasons, analysts have called for increased regional taxes, such as a regional sales tax, which would be used in part to offset the burdens of foregone property tax revenues and of disproportionate numbers of low-income families (Rosentraub et al., 1996).

Other examples of city-county consolidation include Nashville–Davidson County, Jacksonville–Duval County, Lexington–Fayette County, Nashville–Davidson County, and Anchorage–Anchorage Borough. All of these have been fiscally and economically successful, while also making some strides in regard to equitable service provision (Ladd and Yinger, 1991). Other examples of metropolitan government include the Greater

Portland Metropolitan Service District and the Twin Cities Metropolitan Council in Minneapolis–St. Paul.

Few new regional governments have been created; during the 1980s, only six of twenty-seven city-county consolidation efforts were approved by voters (Vogel, 1997, p. 189). They remain politically controversial both because of a somewhat mixed record of accomplishments, and because of the vested interests of local politicians. A case study of Charlotte–Mecklenburg County, North Carolina, illustrates these issues well (Mead, 1997). There, several key factors led to the latest failure to obtain voter approval. As in many other places, the central city minority population and politicians feared that consolidation would dilute their power, and that funding would flow disproportionately to the suburban areas. Also, many public service delivery functions had already been consolidated. Thus there was neither a sense of crisis nor the expectation of great savings from further governmental consolidation. This points to a troublesome dilemma: in areas with the greatest disparities and the least cooperation, there is unlikely to be sufficient trust and experience of collaboration to make consolidation an option; once such collaboration exists, however, complete merger of governmental units may no longer be seen as necessary. These types of concerns—limited efficiencies, loss of political power for minorities, and disproportionate focus on suburban infrastructure rather than central city social and educational problems—recur throughout the literature on metropolitan governance in other places as well (Savitch and Vogel, 1996).

Another method of expanding the reach of local government is through annexation; over the past forty years, central cities in total have doubled in area through this method. Rusk (1993) claims that cities that have annexed surrounding areas have done better, both fiscally and economically, than other cities. However, annexation has happened mostly in rapidly growing areas dominated by their central cities, primarily in the South and West. In other parts of the country, where true deconcentration is more common, annexation is difficult or even impossible because of resistance by existing municipalities. Also, when annexation or consolidation occurs in already built-up areas, individual towns may opt out, as happened in Indianapolis. It is not surprising that suburbanites choose to remain independent; after all, getting away from the central city was one of their original motivations for moving to the suburbs. Suburbanites continue to want to exclude certain types of households and activities, both for social reasons and to protect their real estate values. They also are not eager to take on the responsibility for the problems of central cities and the accompanying fiscal burdens (Downs, 1994).

In some cases, attempts to merge a central city with its larger region are in reality efforts to create *more* fragmentation of the region. Residents of wealthy areas of Miami supported an unsuccessful 1997 referendum to abolish Miami city government and merge it with surrounding Dade County. This would have made it possible for well-to-do areas within Miami to incorporate themselves as separate cities and thus escape the burden of having to pay for the service and infrastructure needs of lower-income Miami residents (Navarro, 1996).

Because of the difficulties in establishing formal regional governments, there is an increasing emphasis on regional *governance* without regional *government*. Examples of this were discussed in connection with special service and taxing districts. Forms of regional governance can range from coordination among a few local governments to direct control by a single authority over certain functions for a metropolitan areas as a whole. Regardless of how they are organized, regional governance structures have the potential to create a forum for regional dialogue (Rosentraub and Nunn, 1994). It remains to be seen in how many cases these limited forms of coordination will create sufficient capacity to address the issues driving the current interest in regionalism, such as economic disparities, the infrastructure costs of suburban sprawl, and the need for global competitiveness.

Suburban residents and businesses have a real stake in regional approaches. Possibly the most persuasive argument for regionalism rests on the recent finding that suburbs with strong central cities fare better themselves in terms of income and home values (Voith, 1992; Barnes and Ledebur, 1994; Savitch, 1993). These data have not yet permeated public consciousness; they also have been attacked by other analysts (Hill et al., 1995). Other arguments elaborate on this connection in terms of the economic benefits of agglomeration; the enduring importance of the central city for the image of the region as a whole; the regional role of many central city cultural, educational, and medical services; and the importance of the low-skilled central city labor force for suburban manufacturing and service jobs (Cisneros, 1995; Downs, 1994). Whether these benefits outweigh the cost of sharing more of the fiscal burden is an empirical question. Recent research suggests that this may not be the case (Voith, 1998), that is, while suburbanites benefit from expenditures made in the central city, for instance, for infrastructure, the benefits may not be worth it if the suburbanites pay a large share of the costs.

Politically, the obstacles to further development of regional governance are immense, not just because of uncertainty about the fiscal impacts, but because of the issues of power and control. The coalition between central city politicians and the lower-income suburbs that is required to achieve governmental restructuring is difficult to put together. Neither group is likely to give up autonomy voluntarily, except in a serious crisis situation; even then, localities tend to look toward state governments for bailouts. Indeed, one Republican county chairman in suburban Chicago argued in a debate about regionalism that "we already have regional government—it is based in Springfield [the state capital]" (Franzen, 1996). Thus, establishment of new regional governments is likely to be quite limited in the United States.

5.4 CONCLUSIONS

The uneven development and disparities among different parts of the metropolitan region are not simply the result of inevitable market forces or the irresistible logic of the invisible hand. While not masterminded by anyone, they have been the consequence—sometimes intended and sometimes not—of a combination of private decisions and public policies. Even now, agencies such as the Illinois Department of Transportation claim to make decisions on transportation grounds only, without any concern or interest in land use consequences.

Just as public policy has a significant effect on metropolitan deconcentration, it can also be redirected to take into account the negative effects of this process. The analysis presented in this book suggests this can be done without noticeable efficiency losses to the economy as a whole, while garnering large distributional benefits.

In this chapter we have reviewed a range of policies that have an effect on redirecting metropolitan growth. Among the main types of policies are those that directly constrain growth or allocate costs more accurately to those who cause them, policies that redistribute the benefits of growth or deconcentration more equitably, and policies that enhance the efficiency of places that are presently not efficient from a market perspective. Each of these types of policies can be assessed in terms of its contribution to slowing metropolitan deconcentration, its feasibility of implementation both politically and programmatically, and its power to redress inequities within a region. (See table 5-1 for a summary.)

In the first group, impact fees and growth controls are in fairly broad use, while congestion pricing is virtually nonexistent. Expansion of such policies would have beneficial effects in redirecting growth, but there are many side-effects associated with their use. It is not always clear where growth will go instead. Also, the geographic level at which impact fees are collected does not neatly match the area within which impacts occur. Those who bear costs but are located outside the municipality where new development is located have no way to assess impact fees at present. Given the experiences with these policies presented earlier, impact fees appear to be quite desirable, because of both their effect on moderating sprawl and their general feasibility. Growth management also reduces

Table 5-1.

Summary Comparison of Policies

	Effect on Slowing Sprawl	Feasibility	Equity
Impact Fees	+	+	0
Growth Management	+	−	0
Congestion Pricing	0	−	0
Reverse Commutin	−	+	+
Affordable Housing	−	0	+
Special Districts	0	+	+
Tax Sharing	+	−	++
Growth Back to City	+	0	++
Regional Government	+	−−	+

Note: +: positive effect; 0: mixed effect or no effect; −: negative effect.

sprawl, but consistent implementation remains politically difficult. Both of these policies have at best a mixed effect on reducing regional disparities, since they may create and protect well-to-do enclaves. Congestion pricing is elegant from an economist's point of view but appears to have little political viability. In any event, it is unlikely to have a major effect on sprawl, and its effect on equity concerns depends entirely on how its proceeds are used.

The second group of policies attempts to redistribute the benefits of growth and deconcentration through schemes such as tax-base sharing and special taxing districts, or by providing better access to new economic opportunities through reverse commuting or affordable housing strategies. These programs essentially leave the current pattern of deconcentration unchallenged, although the former may slow down sprawl somewhat, while the latter may slightly facilitate it. With the exception of reverse commuting, these programs are controversial because they are seen as directly redistributional, without increasing the size of the pie for everyone. Of the two tax-related programs, special districts have clearly proven their feasibility and are in wide use. More drastic forms of tax-base sharing, such as the Minneapolis–St. Paul system, are unlikely to be feasible in many places. Of the other two programs, reverse commuting is uncontroversial, although implementation is still difficult because of the inherent technical problems in organizing an efficient transportation system for deconcentrated places of employment. The Montgomery County, Maryland, example shows that an affordable suburban housing strategy is possible, but the fact that it has not been replicated indicates that it is politically unpalatable.

The third category of policies aims to enhance the opportunities to produce efficiently in locations where this is now difficult, or to supersede intraregional distinctions entirely by developing forms of regional government. Programs aimed at reinvestment in central city and inner ring suburban neighborhoods intend to take away the disadvantages to firm location and efficient production there. These programs include infrastructure reinvestment and, perhaps most important, educational investment. As our analysis shows, the biggest efficiency advantage to private firms locating in the outer suburbs is the availability of relatively high-skilled low-cost labor, in the form of a large female labor force. If central city and inner suburban neighborhoods could match the skill characteristics of this labor force, one of the major disadvantages of these locations would be removed, which could have a significant effect on sprawl. Similarly, a regional government can reduce the incentives for sprawl by eliminating the fiscal rationales for firms and households to move to the urban fringe, and by imposing regionwide land use and infrastructure planning. Both approaches also enhance equity, as they redistribute resources to the central city. However, their feasibility is problematic. It has been difficult to obtain widespread voter support for regional government. Efforts to draw growth back to the city have not been subject to such direct voter judgments, but have been difficult because of a lack of resources and a lack of political will.

Not surprisingly, there is no magic bullet or panacea to address the problem of metropolitan deconcentration. All of the policies suffer from shortcomings in regard to either their effect on reducing sprawl, their political and programmatic feasibility, or their effect on regional disparities. Nevertheless, four policies appear more promising than others. The first is the utilization of impact fees, especially if they were expanded to the supralocal level, such as counties. The second promising approach is the continued expansion of reverse commuting programs to give city residents access to suburban jobs. The third is the use of special districts to share taxes and services. In addition to their direct benefits, these sharing arrangements may also create the social capital necessary for further collaboration. The fourth promising approach is the effort to redirect growth to the central city.

Without making central places more attractive places to invest, attempts to slow down growth on the suburban fringe run the risk of making the metropolitan area as a whole less competitive. In *Does America Need Cities? An Urban Investment Strategy for National Prosperity* (Persky et al., 1992), we argued for concerted action to jump-start economic growth in central cities. At that time, we did not yet have a full analysis of the relative costs and benefits of central city versus suburban growth. Now that we have a clearer picture of the net costs imposed by the current patterns of deconcentration, it is even more evident that such action directed at older cities is strongly justified on equity grounds and at least not contraindicated by efficiency considerations. This review of policies and programs shows that it is possible to redirect metropolitan growth to benefit the central city, and that an array of programs throughout the metropolitan area can be used for this purpose.

Such an effort can be helped by recent developments at the federal level. The President's Council on Sustainable Development (1997) has recommended that federal policy be aimed at promoting metropolitan-scale policy development. It also proposed the establishment of a Metropolitan Sustainable Development Working Group. The tasks of the latter would be to support pilot programs to encourage metropolitan problem solving, to identify and change federal programs or policies that foster sprawl and urban disinvestment, and to reorient federal programs to encourage multijurisdictional cooperation. In an era when major new federal initiatives are unlikely, proposals such as this one may well be viable, since it calls primarily for pilot efforts, a stimulating role, and a review of the effects of current federal programs. In any event, most of the work to achieve greater metropolitan integration will have to be done at the level of regions themselves.

APPENDIX A1

Calculations

This appendix presents a more formal explanation of the calculations underlying the simulations in the text. Overall we make estimates for six cases or scenarios. The first three are for the electrical equipment plant located in the central city (1), an inner suburb (2), or an outer suburb (3). The last three are for the mixed business services facility located in the central city (4), an inner suburb (5), and an outer suburb (6). Chapters 2 and 3 in the main text concern a comparison of cases 1 and 3. Chapter 4 focuses on comparing cases 4 and 6. The inner suburban scenarios are discussed in appendix A2.

In this appendix basic data for all six cases will be presented together to avoid repetition. For most categories of benefits and costs, the figures presented in the main text are simply calculated as differences between two cases as described in this appendix. For some categories of benefits or costs—in particular, those involving impacts on the rest of the nation— the basic calculations must from the start be carried out in terms of the difference of two cases. In considering such benefits or costs below, we specify formulas applicable for any pair of cases.

A1.1 SITE, RESIDENCE, HOUSEHOLD INCOME, AND GENDER

Throughout the main text we are called on to predict economic behaviors such as commuting. We base these predictions on the expected demographic characteristics of the new employees. We begin by distributing the labor force at the primary site of each scenario by residence, household income, and gender. The basic data are from the Public Use Microdata Sample (PUMS) of the 1990 Census. For each scenario, primary site workers (either manufacturing or services) are distributed across three residence areas (central city, inner suburbs, and outer suburbs), three household income groups (1989 household income < $30,000, $30,000–

$75,000, and > $75,000) and two genders in the same proportions as found in the PUMS for the sum of all workers in that industry at that workplace location. A typical entry for this variable, Pjw,rys, would give the proportion of manufacturing/city workplace employees who are men living in the inner suburbs and coming from a high-income household. The PUMS tells us that for manufacturing as a whole P(j = manufacturing)(w = city),(r = inner)(y = high)(s = male) is equal to 4.8%. Thus in our first scenario the new thousand-worker plant in the city has 4.8% of its labor force in this cell: males living in the inner suburbs with a household income greater than $75,000.

A1.2 THE MULTIPLIER

As mentioned in the text, we used Regional Economic Models, Inc.'s model of the Chicago metropolitan area to assign multiplier jobs to city, inner suburbs, and outer suburbs under each scenario. Six simulations, one for each scenario, of the 1994 version of the REMI model were executed. The REMI model has a distinct advantage over other regional models. It breaks down first-round multiplier effects by subregions and then allows interactions among those subregions. Although the REMI model has four subregions for the Chicago metropolitan area, we aggregate these into three areas: the city proper, the inner suburbs or remainder of Cook County, and the outer suburbs (consisting of Lake, McHenry, DuPage, Kane, and Will Counties).

The output of each simulation gives expected employment changes in the three geographic areas, classified by nine industries. As noted in the main text, the REMI model actually predicts a somewhat higher regional multiplier for an outer suburban siting and a somewhat smaller one for a central city siting. These differences are difficult to rationalize. We rescaled the REMI results to force equality between the multipliers for the three simulations under each industry. The resulting variable, Ljw(K), reports the expected number of employees in industry j and workplace w under scenario K.

Using the same basic methodology as for manufacturing and services, we estimated Pjw,rys, the shares of workers in industry j and workplace w who live in residence area r, are in households with income y and are of sex s. These are the residential and demographic distributions of all workers in secondary industries. As for primary manufacturing or service workers, each industry-workplace is distributed across eighteen demographic types (three residences, three household incomes, and two genders).

By combining information on the geographic-industrial distribution of induced employment, Ljw(K), with the Pjw,rys we can estimate the demographic characteristics (place of residence, household income, and sex) for all workers (direct, indirect, and induced) associated with each case assuming that the average distributions hold at the margin.

More formally we calculate:

1) $\text{Nwrys}(K) = \sum_{j} \text{Pjw,rys} * \text{Ljw}(K)$

where Nwrys(K) is the number of workers under case K who work in w, live in r, and have household income y, and sex s; Pjwrys is the proportion of workers in industry j and workplace w who have residence r, income y, and sex s; and Ljw(K) is the number of workers under case K who are in industry j in workplace w.

Notice that we aggregate across industry groups. We drop industry specificity, since for the purposes of estimating externalities such as traffic congestion or the absorption of open land we have little interest in a worker's industry but considerable interest in his or her income, residence, and sex. In these cases, for the workers at each place of work, we have used the secondary industry identification only as a bridge through the PUMS data to these other variables. However, for some purposes where industry is relevant we maintain industry detail and use Njwrys defined in the obvious way: Pjw,rys*Ljw(K).

As discussed in chapter 2, not all new workers will generate a new household in the metropolitan area. Rather, the number of new households depends on the characteristics of the new workers, their jobs, and their households' other sources of income. In particular, workers accounting for a small share of household income are likely to be drawn from households already residing in the area. Following this logic, we compute from the PUMS sample for each group of workers defined by place of residence/income/gender (rys) the proportion who (1) account for more than two-thirds of their household income (Frys), and (2) account for between one-third and two-thirds of their household income (Grys). For each new worker in the first group we assume a new household is founded. We assume a new household is founded for every two new workers in the second group. All other workers—those accounting for less than one-third of their household income—are assumed to be drawn from existing households. This approach gives equation (2):

2) $\text{Hrys}(K) = \sum_{w} (\text{Frys} + 0.5 * \text{Grys}) * \text{Nwrys}(K),$

where all variables are as previously defined and Hrys(K) is the number of new households under case K which live in place r, have household income y, and have a newly employed worker of sex s. Notice that these estimates include the primary workers as well as the secondary ones.

A1.3 EXTERNALITIES

Congestion

For each of the fifty-four places of work/place of residence/household income/sex groups, we find from PUMS the proportion commuting by automobile, the average number of riders per auto, and the average commuting time per vehicle. From these data we calculate the effective vehicle time/worker (AVwrys) for each place of work/place of residence/household income/sex group. This is calculated as the share using auto multiplied by the mean auto travel time divided by the number of riders per vehicle:

3) $AVwrys = (Swrys * ATwrys)/Rwrys,$

where AVwrys is the effective auto vehicle time per worker for commuters between workplace w and residence r of income y and sex s, Swrys is the share of commuters in group wrys using automobiles, ATwrys is the average one-way automobile commuting time for auto users in group wrys, and Rwrys is the average number of riders per vehicle for group wrys. The AVwrys is presented in the main text in table 2-2. AVwrys represents the additional automobile vehicle minutes that can be expected when a commuter of the given workplace, residence, income level, and sex is added.

For each scenario we then calculate:

4) $D(K) = 8.33 * \sum_{wrys} Avwrys * Nwrys(K)$

where D(K) is the total number of commuting hours per year associated with case K, Nwrys(K) is the number of workers under case K who work in w, live in r, have income y, and have sex s (from equation 1 above); AVwrys is the effective auto vehicle time per worker commuting to workplace w from residence r, having income y and sex s (from equation 3 and table 2-2); and 8.33 is a constant converting one-way minutes per day to total hours per year. The dollar value of the congestion externality is then calculated by simply multiplying D(K) by the estimate in the text of the externality cost of an additional vehicle hour, $10.50.

Accidents

The basic strategy here is to link accidents to expected changes in auto ownership under each scenario and then multiply by an expected accident cost per vehicle. New auto ownership is determined by:

5) $A(K) = \sum_{rys} Vrys * Hrys(K)$

where Hrys(K) is defined above in equation 2 and Vrys is the average number of cars of household group rys. The values of Vrys are estimated from the PUMS. A(K) is turned into dollar costs by multiplying by the average annual accident cost per vehicle discussed in the main text, $425.

Air Pollution

The procedure followed here for air pollution is almost identical to that for accidents. The basic starting point is the same, A(K), the estimated number of new vehicles associated with each case. These are simply multiplied by the air pollution costs per vehicle, $71 per year, to give dollar estimates of air pollution costs.

Open Space

As indicated in the main text, we assume that only new activities located in the outer suburbs reduce open space. We start with nonresidential land absorption. The estimated per employee space requirements by industry, SAj, are combined with each scenario's outer suburban employment by industry to give nonresidential land absorption, NLA(K), according to:

$$6) \qquad NLA(K) = \sum_j SAj * L(w = outer)j(K),$$

where SAj is industry j's absorption per worker and L(w = outer)j(K) is the number of new outer suburban workers in industry j under scenario K.

For residential land absorption, we start with the estimates of the number of new outer suburban households, H(r = outer)ys(K) in each scenario as given by equation 3. From the PUMS data we estimate the proportion, Rtys, of each household type choosing residence category (t).

The three residence categories are multifamily, single detached < 1 acre, and single detached > 1 acre residences. These housing choices absorb on average 0.05 acres, 0.25 acres, and 1.5 acres, respectively. The residential acreage absorbed, RLA(K), then becomes:

$$7) \qquad RLA(K) = \sum_{tys} SBt * Rtys * H(r = outer)ys(K),$$

where SBt is the average acreage absorbed by residences of category t.

Both nonresidential and residential land uses are adjusted upward by 50% to take account of various associated public land uses such as sidewalks, roadways, and parks. We apply a value of $180 per acre per year to monetize the value of the loss of open space.

Housing Abandonment

For each scenario, we start from $Nr(y = \text{low income})sj(K)$, the number of predicted workers by residence, sex, and industry from low-income households. For each $r(y = \text{low income})sj$ group of workers we determine, from the PUMS, the proportion, $Brsj$, who meet both of the following criteria:

1. earned less than $10 per hour in 1989
2. without their earnings, their households would be below the poverty level

Poverty levels are here defined as $7,250 for a one- or two-person household and $12,000 for a three-or-more-person household.

Then for each residential area r our estimate of those households avoiding poverty because of the new facility is just:

8) $$AVOIDr(K) = \sum_{sj} Brsj * Nr(y = \text{low})sj(K).$$

We take the sum of these estimates for the city and inner suburbs, $AVOID(r = \text{city})(K) + AVOID(r = \text{inner})(K)$, since abandonment is not a problem in the outer suburbs. Then, as discussed in the main text, we multiply each of these by 0.27, our estimate of abandonments per poverty household. Finally we turn these abandonments into a dollar figure by using the text estimate of a $1,000 annual externality per abandoned unit.

Spatial Mismatch

From the PUMS we determine the proportion of low-wage workers among those workers in low-income households for each industry/workplace/sex group, jws. Call this $LWw(y = \text{low})sj$. Here we defined low wages as less than $8 per hour in 1989, a somewhat more stringent cutoff than for the discussion of abandonment. Applying this share to the number of low-income workers in each group, $Nw(y = \text{low})sj(K)$, gives the number of low-wage–low-income workers for each group. Summing these gives the total number of low-wage–low-income workers for each case, $LL(K)$.

9) $$LL(K) = \sum_{wsj} LWw(y = \text{low})sj * Nw(y = \text{low})sj(K).$$

Finally using the average annual earnings figure of $12,300 1995 dollars, we calculate the total earnings of these workers. As discussed in the text, the spatial mismatch is calculated at half the difference between cases. For example, the mismatch from comparing scenario m and scenario n would be $(1/2)[LL(K = m) - LL(K = n)]$.

National Externalities

External effects on the rest of the nation vary across scenarios, because those scenarios differ in the number of households of each income group they attract to the Chicago metropolitan area. Formally this difference, $DHy(K = m, K = n)$, between scenario l and scenario m for income group y is defined as:

10) $$DHy(K = m, K = n) = \sum_{rs} Hrys(K = m)$$
$$- \sum_{rs} Hrys(K = n),$$

where $Hrys(K)$ has been defined in equation 2.

The externalities affected by these differences are congestion, other auto-related impacts, and open space. For each income group we use our Chicago PUMS data to determine average congestion costs, other auto-related costs, and value of space absorption per household. For example, for other auto-related costs for the middle income group we calculate:

11) $$(\$425 + \$71) * V(y = middle),$$

where $V(y = middle)$ is the average number of automobiles across all middle-income households in the Chicago metropolitan area. Summing across these three externalities gives an average externality cost per household of a given income group, ECy.

We assume that those drawn to the area or pushed out of the area under alternative scenarios would impose externalities elsewhere roughly equal to the average for their income group in the Chicago area. Multiplying each $DHy(K = m, K = n)$ by the appropriate ECy and summing over income groups gives the estimates of national externalities used in the text.

A1.4 PUBLIC-SECTOR IMPACTS

Residential

Starting with residential revenues from the 1987 Census of Governments, the share of state and federal contributions and nonresidential revenues as estimated below are subtracted. While state and federal transfers are revenues to local governments, they are essentially subsidies from higher level of governments. We take the overall intragovernmental subsidy to the metropolitan area as a given, independent (except for highway and housing subsidies noted below) of the geographic distribution of the area's population. The remaining figure is divided by total households to give a per household average revenue. In what follows we assume that new low-income households (< $30,000) generate only 80% of this figure while middle-income households generate 100% and high-income households (> $75,000) generate 170%. These estimates are based on PUMS data on property taxes paid by homeowners in each of the categories in each of the areas.

On the expenditure side, we first deduct estimated expenditures for nonresidential uses (see below) from total expenditures. Since in what follows we need disaggregated figures by broad types of expenditures, the nonresidential figure must be apportioned among these various types of expenditures. Clearly little if any nonresidential expenditures are undertaken for education, public welfare, hospitals, health, parks and recreation, and housing and community development. The nonresidential expenditures are then divided among the remaining categories (police, fire, sewerage, sanitation, administration, and interest) in proportion to their relative importance in local expenditures.

For each category we estimate marginal expenditures on new households as a fixed proportion of average expenditures. These estimates are based on an informal review of city services in Chicago. In the simulations new city residents add nothing to public welfare, housing and community development, interest, and sewerage. For administration, libraries, other transit (nonhighways), and parks and recreation we take the marginal cost in the city to be 25% of the average. (Note that highway expenditures, with their substantial state and federal subsidies, are considered separately in the next section.) For all other categories of expenditures except education we set new resident costs at half the city's average cost.

With respect to education, we differentiate among city households in terms of their income levels. In the city a new low-income household adds 120% of average public school costs per household, while a middle-income household adds 100%. A high-income household adds only 40%. These estimates are based on 1990 public school enrollment figures by household income obtained from the PUMS sample.

For outer suburban households we take marginal cost as equal to average cost less public welfare. By their very nature as growing communities, these outer suburbs have little if any excess capacity. In addition we make a correction for the increasingly common use of impact fees. Currently impact fees in the most rapidly growing residential areas in the outer suburbs range up to $10,000 per dwelling, but not all areas are so aggressive. In what follows we assume that impact fees in the outer suburbs average $8,000 per new household. On an annual basis (at 5% per year) this reduces per household expenditures by $400.

Presumably, marginal costs in the inner suburbs form an intermediate case between the city and outer suburbs. Some of these municipalities are themselves losing population and can easily accommodate new households. Others are still growing and thus are hard-pressed to expand public capital and service systems. With some uncertainty, we estimate marginal expenditures in these suburbs as a whole to be 50% of average expenditures, except for education; the latter, as in the central city, we estimate at 75%.

Subtracting the marginal expenditure figure from the average revenue estimate for each residence and income group gives the net per household fiscal impacts by residence and household income, FHry, as presented in table 2-8.

To estimate the overall net fiscal impact (FHT) we just multiply the number of expected new households by income and residence under each scenario (from equation 2) as follows:

12) $\quad \text{FHT}(K) = \sum_{ry} [\text{FHry} * \sum_{ws} \text{Hrys}(K)]$

Nonresidential

On the revenue side, we make the basic assumption that nonresidential revenues from property taxes, utilities, and fees are proportional to the nonresidential share of total assessed value as reported in the 1987 Census. The 1987 Census was the last one to report revenues by the residential/nonresidential distinction. This allows us to calculate a nonresidential revenue per dollar of nonresidential assessed value. This ratio is taken to apply to new businesses. At the margin, we assume that new employers will have the same average assessment-to-employee ratio as old employers for the three geographic areas.

Thus we estimate:

13) $\quad \text{NREw} = \text{NAw} * \text{REVw}/\text{Ew},$

where NREw is the nonresidential revenue per employee in location w, NAw is the nonresidential share of assessments in location w, REVw is the total revenue in w, and Ew is the total employment in w.

These figures can then be combined with the geographic distribution of employment as estimated by the REMI model for the two scenarios:

14) $\quad \text{NRw}(K) = \text{NREw} * \sum_{j} \text{Ljw}(K),$

where NRw(K) is the nonresident revenue generated in location w under scenario K.

As noted in the text, we take an across-the-board estimate that nonresidential service requirements amount to 60% of nonresidential revenues. This gives the nonresidential expenditure levels under each scenario. Then the net nonresidential surpluses, NSw(K), are just the difference of revenues and expenditures or, given the 60% assumption,

15) $NSw(K) = (1 - 0.6) * NRw(K).$

Subsidies

Highway Subsidies

As suggested in the text, we estimate an annual per vehicle subsidy of $208. We assume that each new vehicle in the metropolitan area receives this average subsidy. The new vehicle estimates A(K) are from equation 6 above.

Housing Subsidies

First, we determine for each of eighteen of our demographic groups (three residences, three income levels, two sexes) what proportion of new households will own their dwellings, HOrys, and what the average value of those dwellings will be, HVrys. These data are taken from the PUMS. The tax avoided by homeowners of each type is estimated by assuming a 5% return on the average value and then multiplying by the marginal tax rate appropriate for this household income, TAXy.

We estimate the tax subsidy associated with each case as follows:

16) $TS(K) = \sum_{rys} 0.05 * Hrys(K) * HOrys * HVrys * TAXy,$

where Hrys(K) is the number of new households at place of residence r, income level y with a worker of sex s employed as a result of case K (from equation 2); HOrys is the proportion of households of type rys who own their homes, HVrys is the average value of those homes, and TAXy is the tax rate appropriate to household income level y.

The Rest of the Nation

We assume that net fiscal surpluses by income group and city/suburban residence are identical in the rest of the country to those in the Chicago metropolitan area. For each income group we calculate an average net surplus, FHy, based on its geographic distribution in the Chicago area, and assume this will hold elsewhere for that income group. These averages just weight the fiscal surpluses by the proportion of that income group living in city, inner suburbs, and outer suburbs:

17) $FH = \sum_r IGry * FHry,$

where the FHry again come from table 2-8 and the proportions of each income group by geographic area (IGry) are taken from the PUMS. These averages are −$644 for low-income households, $221 for middle-income households, and $3,180 for high-income households.

We then multiply each $DHy(K = m, K = n)$ by the appropriate FHy to give estimates of the local fiscal impact on the rest of the country. Notice these numbers can be either negative or positive, depending on whether the rest of the nation bears a greater cost under $K = m$ or under $K = n$.

We follow the exact same steps in estimating the change in housing subsidies for the rest of the nation. In this case the average by income group is $594 for low-income, $1,475 for middle-income, and $2,694 for high-income.

For highway subsidies only changes in outer suburban residents in the rest of the country have an efficiency effect. We estimate these as equal to the outer suburban share, $IG(r = outer)y$, for each income group times the change for that income group between two cases, $DHy(K = m, K = n)$. This number of households is then multiplied by the average vehicles per that income group Vy. For each of these outer suburban vehicles in the rest of the country we take the subsidy to be the average $208 per year. Hence the total change in subsidy is given by:

18) $\sum_y Vy * IG(r = outer)y * DHy(K = m, K = n).$

A1.5 PRIVATE BENEFITS AND COSTS, RESIDENT BENEFITS AND COSTS

As discussed in the main text, the key to measuring resident benefits and costs is to determine the number of workers who maintain their residence in the face of increasing or decreasing travel costs. The "committed stayers" are the ones whose intramarginal welfare levels are affected. Presumably those who change residence are approximately maintaining their welfare at the margin.

For each pair of scenarios, $K = m$, $K = n$, we determine for each residence, sex, and income group the number of "committed stayers." If we compare a facility location in the city to one in the outer suburbs, then the city committed stayers are those who maintain city residence under the outer suburban scenario, but now commute to the outer suburbs. These committed city residents will face a longer commute. On the other hand, we can estimate the number of outer suburban residents who now enjoy a shorter commute. These are the gainers.

To estimate these committed stayers for a given rys group, we use the following type of equation. This one is for a comparison between the city scenario and the outer suburb scenario.

19) $\text{CSrys}(K = \text{city}, K = \text{outer}) = \text{MIN}(|N(w = \text{city})\text{rys}$
$(K = \text{city}) - N(w = \text{city})\text{rys}(K = \text{outer})|, |N(w = \text{outer})$
$(K = \text{city}) - N(w = \text{outer})\text{rys}(K = \text{outer})|),$

which is the minumum (between w = city and w = outer) of the absolute values of the change (across the two scenarios) in the number of rys workers working in w. The assumption is that this minimum change is "taken out" of the larger absolute changes. To get the sense of this approach, consider the following example. When we compare an outer suburban manufacturing site to a central city one, we find that for male low-income city residents there is a decrease of 169 city jobs held and an increase of 20 outer suburban jobs held. We assume that the 20 outer suburban jobholders under the outer suburban scenario would have held city jobs under the city scenario. Hence this minimum change becomes a measure of "committed stayers" for this group. The rest of the loss of 169 city resident/city jobholders either changed workplaces within the metropolitan area or left the area entirely.

The dollar value of the difference in travel time for the "committed stayers" between their original workplace and their new workplace is the measure of gain or loss. The value of travel time is here set at one-third of wages. Wages are estimated as $10 per hour for the low-income group, $20 for the middle-income group, and $40 for the high-income group. Since our income categories are based on household income, we adjust these for the share a worker contributes to his or her household income. Workers accounting for more than two-thirds of household income are set on average at 83% of the full wage, those accounting for between one-third and two-thirds are set at 50%, and for those contributing one-third or less the figure is 17%.

Working through these fairly laborious calculations gives the gain or loss per worker in each committed stayer group, $\text{RGrys}(w = m, w = n)$. The overall estimate of resident commuting gains then follows from the following calculation:

20) $\text{TRCG}(K = m, K = n) = \sum_{\text{rys}} \text{CSrys}(K = m, K = n)*$
$\text{RGrys}(w = m, w = n).$

A similar set of calculations allows us to determine the wage losses of the "committed stayers" once we know the wage differential between each pair of workplaces, WDgrys.

21) $$\text{TRWL}(K = m, K = n) = \sum_{rys} \text{CSrys}(K = m, K = n) *$$
$$\text{WDgrys}(w = m, w = n).$$

The sum of TRCG and TRWL yield the net resident benefits.

Land/Structures

The losses to city and inner suburban structure owners are estimated at $25,000 per abandoned unit. The number of units was estimated above. Again, this figure is annualized at 5% to give an estimate of private costs of abandonment under alternative scenarios.

Business Gains and Losses

Wage Costs

Business gains from reduced wages are estimated from regression equations that explain the logarithm of wages as a function of numerous personal variables and workplace location. One equation is made for men and one for women. The equations are given in table A1-1.

The wage equations make it possible to estimate the total wage bills for each scenario. In doing this we simply calculate:

22) $$\text{WB}(K) = \sum_{wi} \text{Wwj} * \text{Ljw}(K)$$

where Ljw(K) is the number of workers in industry j located in workplace w under scenario K; Wwj is the estimated annual wage in industry j and workplace w. This estimate is based on average annual industry wages for men and women, W(city)sj, taken from PUMS for the central city. In particular we calculate:

23) $$\text{Wwj} = \sum_{s} \text{Dws} * \text{W(city)sj} * \text{Msj},$$

where Dws is the percentage discount from the estimated equations for workplace w and sex s and Msi are metropolitan shares by sex for industry j. In effect this estimated wage holds the proportions of men and women and of the various skill categories constant between areas. If we had just used the actual wages for each location we might have been comparing different quality labor forces.

The final complication is to adjust the estimate of WB(K) for that portion which simply reduces the local price level and is not passed on to business employers. We take this to include all of retail wages and three-eighths of service wages. These are simply subtracted from WB(K).

TABLE A1-1.

Determinants of Wages for Men and Women in
Metropolitan Chicago

	MEN		WOMEN	
	Coefficient	*t*	*Coefficient*	*t*
Intercep	0.27642	9.015	0.8795	21.294
Pow2	−0.01439	−2.739	−0.06889	−12.248
Pow3	−0.02407	−4.332	−0.09621	−16.311
Black	−0.15546	−21.9	−0.0199	−3.017
Hisp	−0.02739	−3.384	−0.04553	−5.42
Ed2	0.091709	7.8	0.048449	3.239
Ed3	0.175071	15.796	0.129159	9.207
Ed4	0.226552	20.171	0.207462	14.567
Ed5	0.371573	30.465	0.378062	25.143
Ed6	0.538316	40.591	0.547376	33.345
Born	0.09414	10.366	0.044589	4.635
Part	0.080241	8.434	−0.03136	−5.051
Lang	0.114679	12.963	0.033238	3.719
Dis	−0.16051	−12.497	−0.09126	−6.199
Age	0.070829	63.694	0.045982	41.52
Agesq	−0.00069	−54.635	−0.00047	−35.943
Vet	−0.01637	−2.695	−0.01039	−0.378
Married	0.190616	36.764	−0.00558	−1.12
Rrelchld	−0.10525	−5.121	−0.09877	−4.891
	+ 22 Occupational dummies		+ 22 Occupational dummies	
	Adj-R2 = 0.34		Adj-R2 = 0.24	

Note: Dependent variable is the logarithm of the hourly wage. POW2 = inner suburban workplace, POW3 = outer suburban workplace, ED2 = less than high school, ED3 = high school degree, ED4 = some college, ED5 = college degree, ED6 = graduate work, BORN = Born in the United States, PART = worked part-time, LANG = English is native language, DIS is disability, AGE = age in years, AGESQ = square of age, VET = veteran status, MARRIED = married, RRELCHLD = related child in household. All data taken from PUMS.

Land Costs and Business Taxes

Land cost savings and business tax savings are treated much like wage savings. Once land costs are determined by industry under each scenario, we adjusted these totals downward for the portion in retailing (all) and services (three-eighths) that are passed along to local consumers.

The local benefit of the nonresidential surplus of taxes paid over public expenditures is a cost to businesses, and thus included here as a private cost. As we did for wage savings, we adjusted this amount for the portions in retailing (all) and services (three-eighths) that are passed along to local consumers.

Construction Costs

We use an estimate of $30,000 construction expenditures per new employee. As noted in the main text, we estimate that suburban construction allows a 12.5% savings. This means a capital savings of $3,750 or annualized at 5% per year about $187.50 savings per worker per year. This is a gain for inner and outer suburban businesses, but a loss for construction workers. In the efficiency analysis this just cancels out.

A1.6 DISTRIBUTION

All costs and benefits were allocated across our three household income groups (low and moderate, less than $30,000; middle, greater than $30,000, but less than $75,000; and high, more than $75,000) and also by geographic area (city, inner suburbs, and outer suburbs). For many of the categories considered we first calculated a joint distribution for income, geography, and sex. Then we simply aggregated across sex and one or the other categories of income and geography to give the simple distributions shown in the text.

Externalities

Congestion and Auto-Related

From the 1990 PUMS, we first calculated the total auto commuting time for each rys group in the metropolitan area as a whole,

24) $ATrys * Srys * Erys,$

where Erys is the number of workers in the metropolitan area living in residence r in households of income y and gender s, Srys is the average share of rys workers who commute by auto, and ATrys is the average auto commuting time of those rys workers. One possibility was to just use these total auto commuting times for the distribution of congestion costs, but instead we weighted by average household income levels, Yrys, for reasons discussed in the text. This gave the following weights:

25) $(ATrys * Srys * Erys * Yrys)/\sum_{rys} (ATrys * Srys * Erys * Yrys).$

These rys weights were aggregated first by gender and then by residence or income to give the three-way distributions used in the text.

We assume that all other auto-related externalities fall randomly on the metropolitan population. Again, since the valuation of these externalities is likely to be proportional to household income we use income shares to distribute the burden across rys groups. As for congestion, these disaggregated figures are summed over genders and then either geography or income groups to give the income and geographic distributions in the text.

Open Space

The open space externality is distributed by income shares in the same manner as the auto-related externalities.

Abandonment

Geographically the abandonment externality follows the poverty population affected by one or the other facility sitings. The key estimates here are the numbers of households from city and inner suburbs that are kept from poverty under each scenario, AVOIDr(K), from equation 8 above. Taking the difference between each pair of scenarios, $K = m$ and $K = n$, allows the calculation of the geographic distribution of the externality for each comparison.

For the income distribution of this externality we follow the approach discussed in the main text. Low-income renters are assumed to escape the abandonment externality. Since about 64% of low-income households were renters in 1990, only 36% of the externality is assumed to fall on low-income households. The rest of the externality is divided equally between high- and middle-income households, presumably in line with their ownership of low-income rental units.

Mismatch

The procedure used to distribute the mismatch externality is fully described in the text.

National Externalities

Obviously these costs or benefits fall geographically on those outside the region as a whole. As to income distribution, we assume that the burden of each type of externality is distributed across income groups nationally in the same manner as determined for that type of externality in the metropolitan area.

Public Subsidies

Local Fiscal Impacts

In the calculations above we have derived the geographical distribution of both residential and nonresidential local surpluses.

For the income distribution of the local surpluses we first calculate the income distributions of each geographic area, SHAREry, as we did for the income distribution of all other auto-related externalities above. From here it is a simple matter to reallocate the geographic shares to income groups:

$$26) \quad \text{SHAREy} = \sum_y \text{SHAREry} * \text{SHAREr},$$

where SHAREy is the share of the y income group, SHAREr is the share of the r residential group, and SHAREry is the y income share of the r residential group.

National Subsidies

These fall almost exclusively on taxpayers outside the area. By income group we assume that they will be borne proportionately to income shares. We assume the national shares by income group are the same as the metropolitan ones.

Private Benefits

Resident Gains

From the calculations for equation (20) and equation (21) we have the resident gains and losses for each rys group. These are aggregated first by gender then by geography or income group to give the distribution of gains by income group and geography.

All Other Categories

The procedures used for distributing the remaining private benefits and costs—abandonment, wage costs, business taxes, and construction costs—are fully described in the main text.

APPENDIX A2

The Inner Suburbs

In the main text, we contrasted the impacts of economic development in the central city and outer suburbs; we have considered inner suburbs only as residential locations and secondary employment sites, not as potential sites for primary facilities. It seems only reasonable to consider how primary sites at inner suburban locations compare to those in the city proper and those at the periphery.

Increasingly, inner suburbs face many of the same problems as the central city. Where jobs were once abundant, these suburbs now face increasing competition from newer areas closer to the periphery; some inner suburbs have experienced wholesale deindustrialization. As is the case in the central city, presumably these trends are rooted in the profit calculus of the individual firms involved. In response, many inner suburbs have aggressively entered the competition to encourage local economic development.

It would have been misleading to use statistical averages for all suburbs to analyze the consequences of employment deconcentration. Nevertheless, the inner suburbs are of interest in their own right. How does an inner suburban location compare in overall efficiency to a location in the city or outer suburbs? And beyond efficiency, what are the distributional consequences of inner suburban development? To address these questions, we use the same basic methods of analysis as in the text proper. Thus in what follows, we summarize our findings with little reference to method.

As we have done so far, we define the inner suburbs as Cook County outside Chicago proper. Although these suburbs vary considerably in the extent and nature of their economic activity as well as in their demographics, our major data sources (the PUMS and the REMI model) do not allow a finer geographic breakdown. Thus the estimates below are averages across a diverse group of municipalities.

A2.1 INNER SUBURBS AND MANUFACTURING EXTERNALITIES

Siting the electrical equipment plant in suburban Cook County gives rise to an externality pattern largely similar to that generated if the outer suburban site is chosen. The most significant finding is that a primary siting in the inner suburbs generates greater automobile-related congestion than one in the outer suburbs. Both central city and outer suburban commuters to the inner suburbs must depend almost exclusively on automobiles. The accident and air pollution externalities are almost identical to those in the outer suburbs.

The other major externality in the inner suburbs, labor mismatch, looks very similar to that in the outer suburbs. This finding is perhaps more surprising than the previous one. Since the inner suburbs contain many low-income households, one might have expected a better performance on the mismatch externality. However, it seems that a large share of low-wage jobs in these suburbs go to members of middle- and high-income households. Very likely, the actual outcome would depend on the precise location of the plant in the inner suburbs. Since these suburbs vary dramatically in their demographic composition, the hypothetical based on average figures may not provide a good summary.

Taking all externalities together, the plant in the inner suburbs creates $1.25 million more in externalities than in the central city, and about $140,000 more than in the outer suburbs.

Public-Sector Costs

Nonresidential revenues per dollar of nonresidential assessment are about the same in the inner suburbs as in the outer ring: 6%. This is considerably lower than the central city figure of 14%. Under the inner suburban siting, however, a greater proportion of the multiplier effect spills over into the central city, generating modest employment growth there and hence nonresidential tax collections at the higher city rate. Together, these factors imply that nonresidential surpluses under inner suburban siting of the plant take a value intermediate between those associated with central city placement and those associated with outer suburban placement.

Inner suburban residential revenues per household for all income levels lie between the corresponding figures for central city and outer suburban households. On the expenditure side, our estimates suggest about the same cost per new inner suburban household as per new outer suburban household. Inner suburbs have lower marginal costs relative to average cost, but somewhat higher average costs than the outer suburbs. Hence the overall expenditure per new household is about the same. Again, the central city has an even lower figure, because at the margin it requires little investment to handle increased population. On net, the surpluses generated by all income levels in the inner suburbs lie intermediate between the corresponding figures for the central city and outer suburbs. Since under the inner suburban plant siting, relatively more new households locate in the inner suburbs, the residential losses of net surplus (relative to the central city) are less for this case than for the outer suburban case.

Both highway subsidies and owner-occupied subsidies closely resemble those generated from the outer suburban siting. Similarly, the public-sector costs generated elsewhere in the nation as a result of the inner suburban siting are about equal to those of the greenfield location.

In sum, then, locating the electrical equipment plant in the inner suburbs imposes public-sector costs about $820,000 greater than the same plant in the central city. This is better than the outer suburbs, where the same plant leads to public-sector costs more than $1.5 million greater than in the central city.

Private Benefits

The inner suburban case generates a slightly greater resident welfare loss than the outer suburban one. This is because so many inner suburban residents work in the central city. Locating a plant in inner suburbs as opposed to the central city allows these residents to reduce their commuting time, but weighs heavily on their wages. Land cost and business tax savings are also less at the inner suburb location.

Like central city development, inner suburban expansion helps limit housing abandonment, but here the net effect is somewhat smaller. This is a relatively small number and hence has only a limited effect overall.

The important private benefits are wage savings, land cost savings, and business taxes. For each of these the inner suburban location generates a result intermediate between central city and outer suburb. On taxes, the primary inner suburban placement saves the expanding businesses (with the exception of retail and personal services) about $260,000 over the central city siting, but costs $230,000 more than the outer suburban scenario.

Wage savings behave similarly. After we deduct retail and local services (see section 2.4 above), we find that businesses save almost $1.3 million over the central city case, but must spend more than $600,000 over the outer suburban case. Land costs in the inner suburb scenario are

$300,000 better than the city scenario, but about $300,000 greater than the outer suburban scenario.

Adding all private benefits, the inner suburban scenario yields gains of about $1.4 million over the central city. But the inner suburban siting still runs about $1.2 million short of the outer suburban scenario.

Net Effects

In terms of overall social welfare, the inner suburban sites perform worse than both the central city and the outer suburbs (see table A2–1). When compared with the central city, the inner suburbs show strong private benefits but much higher externalities and public-sector costs.

In comparison with the outer suburbs, the inner suburbs show a similar performance on externalities, do better on public-sector costs, and do worse on private benefits.

Distribution

Here we summarize the major distributional implications of choosing an inner suburban site for the electrical equipment plant rather than a central city site. Consider first the income distributions of these changes. All of the externalities generated are distributed across household income groups in the same manner as for the central city–outer suburban comparison in chapter 3. Similarly, the income distributions of the private benefits remain the same. The only change is in the income distribution of the local public-sector costs. These shift somewhat toward higher-income households. Overall, the total distribution still strongly favors higher-income households, which as a group benefit absolutely by about

TABLE A2-1.

Costs and Benefits of Inner Suburban Development of an Electrical Equipment Plant

	Inner Suburban Site Relative to Central City Site	Inner Suburban Site Relative to Outer Suburban Site
1. Externalities	−1263	−142
2. Public-Sector Costs	−820	+727
3. Private Benefits	1432	−1166
Total	−652	−580

Note: All figures in thousands of 1995 dollars; (−) indicates inner suburban site generates a cost relative to alternative site.

$900,000 per year. But the basic inefficiency of this shift leaves low- and middle-income households losing more than $1.5 million per year.

From a geographic perspective, there are two main changes. First, both mismatch and abandonment costs fall even more heavily on the central city, while the inner suburbs that receive the new plant actually improve. Second, public-sector costs now shift completely to the city, with the inner suburbs actually benefiting from the nonresidential taxes. In terms of total impacts, the rest of the nation again makes out well with a gain of more than $1.7 million, but at a high cost to city households, which lose more than $2.0 million. Inner suburban households lose slightly, while outer suburban households lose about $340,000 per year. This latter result largely reflects the increase in outer suburban congestion, which in this case is not offset by tax revenues from the primary facility.

A2.2 INNER SUBURBS AND BUSINESS SERVICES

In considering the inner suburbs as a possible location for a business services facility, our estimates show that they generate an overall welfare impact inferior to that of either the city or the outer suburbs. In particular, a business services facility gives rise to fewer private benefits in the inner suburbs than it does in the outer suburbs. This comparison is essentially the same as for the electrical equipment plant. The inner suburban site for a business service facility performs worse than the central city with respect to both externalities and public costs.

Externalities

The inner suburban location generates somewhat greater congestion externalities than the outer suburban one. But these costs in both locations are considerably greater than in the central city. With respect to the second large externality, labor mismatch, the inner suburb scenario produces greater costs than the central city but somewhat lower ones than the outer suburbs.

In regard to accidents and air pollution, there are almost no differences among the three scenarios. Outer suburban siting uses up a bit more open space than either the city or inner suburban site. Similarly, either a city or inner suburban site will slow housing abandonment a bit more than an outer suburban site. All of these noncongestion externalities are small because of the relatively low number of new households generated by business service expansion under any of the scenarios.

Placing the business services facility in the inner suburbs rather than the central city modestly raises externalities experienced in the rest of the nation as low-income households failing to find city jobs eventually leave the region. In this respect an inner suburban location is much like an outer suburban site.

In total, locating the business services facility in the inner suburbs generates $830,000 more in externalities than locating it in the central city. However, this is still a bit less than the externalities that are associated with an outer suburban site.

Public-Sector Costs

An inner suburban siting will produce both nonresidential and residential fiscal surpluses. The size of these fiscal gains is intermediate between those achieved under city and outer suburban scenarios. There is little difference among suburban scenarios with respect to highway subsidies. An inner suburban location, however, requires a somewhat larger housing subsidy than an outer suburban one. Public-sector subsidies required elsewhere in the nation are somewhat less with an inner suburban location than with an outer suburban one.

In sum, an inner suburban location demands some $666,000 more subsidies than a city location, but about $200,000 less than an outer suburban location.

Private Benefits

The main private benefit of locating the business services facility in the inner suburbs as opposed to the central city again takes the form of reduced wage costs. This gain stands at close to $1.4 million—a sizable sum, but still considerably less than the almost $2.0 million gain associated with locating the facility in the outer suburbs.

The next largest private benefit relates to tax gains in the inner suburb as opposed to central city. An inner suburban location leads to tax savings of $255,000 relative to the central city. However, compared to the outer suburbs, inner suburban taxes are still high.

Adding up the private benefits puts the inner suburban case about $1.4 million ahead of the central city case, but $900,000 behind the outer suburban case. This result is almost identical to that for the electrical equipment plant. This similarity actually represents the netting out of two differences. The multiplier for the business services facility is considerably smaller than that for the electrical equipment plant. This lower multiplier implies lower total wage savings from deconcentration. On the other hand, the business services facility employs a larger proportion of women than the electrical equipment plant. By taking a suburban location, this facility takes greater advantage of the larger city–suburban wage differential for women.

Net Effects

Table A2-2 presents the summary statement for inner suburban development of a business services facility. The inner suburban scenario produces an efficiency loss in comparison with the central city site or the outer suburban site.

Distribution

Again, we limit our comments to comparing the central city–outer suburban shift to the central city–inner suburban shift. In terms of the income distribution of the changes, the pattern is similar to that which we observed for the electrical equipment plant. In comparison to a central city location, the inner suburban site imposes costs on low- and middle-income households amounting to about $1 million.

The geographical distributions now show modest gains in the inner suburbs, as low-wage workers from low-income inner suburban households find employment. But these are, as always, far less than the losses of city workers. In total, the basic pattern emerges of a large transfer from the city to the rest of the nation which gains $1.6 million.

TABLE A2-2.

Costs and Benefits of Inner Suburban Development of a Business Services Facility

	Inner Suburban Site Relative to Central City Site	Inner Suburban Site Relative to Outer Suburban Site
1. Externalities	−829	+72
2. Public-Sector Costs	−666	+206
3. Private Benefits	1390	−898
Total	−105	−620

Note: All figures in thousands of 1995 dollars; (−) indicates inner suburban site generates a cost relative to alternative site.

APPENDIX A3

Basic Theory

The simplest version of the monocentric model of urban location theory takes all households as having identical tastes and incomes with all employment located at the center of the urban area. Those households living farther from the center face higher commuting costs, but are compensated by lower land prices. In equilibrium all households enjoy the same level of welfare.

When decentralized workplace locations are introduced into this model, workers taking jobs farther from the center are willing to accept lower wages because living nearby, they can save on both land costs and commuting costs. Firms staying at the center enjoy urban agglomeration economies large enough to compensate for higher labor costs. In the new equilibrium all households again enjoy the same level of welfare.

Consider in this simplest possible metropolitan area the implications of a single firm deciding on a central city or a suburban location. Since this individual firm is quite small relative to the size of the metropolitan economy, its siting will have no significant effect on the market prices of land or labor in any location. More formally, the bid-rent function and the wage gradient remain constant, regardless of the firm's decision. The firm can take prices as givens.

Now assume the firm is not strongly bound to the city by agglomeration economies. Then with a city location it will face relatively high wage and land costs. If the firm chooses the suburbs, its wage costs will be lower. Its land costs will also be lower. These are real efficiency gains passed on in either higher profits or lower prices for the firm's product. The workers are fundamentally indifferent between the two cases. With a central location for the firm, worker households will be stretched out between the center and the periphery of the metropolitan area. Each household receives the same exact welfare level. If the firm chooses the suburbs, then all households will live farther out than the firm because land costs are assumed to be lower as one moves farther out. Wages will be lower, but so will commuting times. Welfare of the workers will be essentially unchanged. Other metropolitan area residents are not significantly affected by the firm's decision.

This simple model gives the essence of the laissez-faire argument for decentralization. Many who take the laissez-faire position realize that the real world is more complex. However, they hold that the complexities and counterforces of the real world are not sufficient to offset the efficiency gains generated by the forces described here. This claim is fundamentally an empirical one. In the first instance, the question is whether negative externalities and public costs associated with a more peripheral workplace location (and paid by the metropolitan area as a whole) might outweigh the firm's reduction in wage and land costs and any other private cost savings associated with such a location. This is a central question addressed in the main text.

Notice, introducing externalities or amenities into the model, in itself, has no effect on the proposition that, within a given scenario, all workers' households enjoy the same welfare level. Since all households are identical, the equal welfare condition must still be met. Any negative externalities or positive amenities must be "shared" equally. If those externalities or amenities are metropolitan-wide, then the result is straightforward. However, if they are linked only to one locality or a group of localities within the metro area, they must be fully offset by differences in land costs. The land market works to equalize welfare. In particular, this model predicts that changes in externalities or amenities fall no more heavily on city than on suburb. Notice, the point here is not one of efficiency, but of equity. The externality for example may be at a nonoptimal level, but it falls evenly on all metropolitan households.

An obvious problem with this simple scenario is the fact that households differ considerably in terms of income-generating skills. Since we are interested in distributional consequences of decentralization as well as questions of efficiency, we must expand our theoretical treatment to include these differences in human capital. Allowing this complexity into the model requires that welfare now be equalized within each household skill/real income group, but not across groups. With differing consumption patterns across groups, we can easily observe differences across groups in the impacts of externalities. If richer families commute by auto and poorer ones take the subway, then increases in road congestion will fall on the former and not on the latter. Similarly, if the underlying maximizing decisions by households put a higher proportion of one income class or another into the central city, then changes in externality and amenity levels may well have differential impacts induced by differences based on income.

In addition to skill differences, we know households differ considerably in their taste for city and suburban living. The existence of such taste differences implies that welfare levels between city and suburban households, even those of the same basic income level, do not have to equalize on average. As a result, most households who "like the city" will remain city dwellers even if negative externalities increase slightly in the city. Similarly, households attached to "suburban lifestyles" will absorb welfare losses associated with small increases in negative externalities there.

For a substantial number of households, the firm specificity of its skills and the strength of its residential preferences may be so substantial as to greatly reduce the options available. The complicated commuting patterns we actually observe are best explained in terms of households with "entanglements" at both their place of residence and their place of work. Thus a household may be bound to a neighborhood by friendships and community ties, while its chief wage earner may continue a difficult commute because he or she earns a premium at work based on specialized human capital not easily transferred to a more conveniently located employer. At any given time, many, perhaps most households will be less than fully mobile.

For a given skill/income group, then, only households whose tastes and job mobility leave them "at the margin" between alternative locations will experience welfare equalization. But these marginal households in each skill category are quite important. Their perceptions of alternative bundles of wages, rents, commuting, externalities, taxes, and public goods play the key role in establishing spatial equilibrium.

Now consider again our basic problem of alternative locations for an employer. Perhaps the easiest way to visualize the theoretical argument is to think in term of an employer relocating from city to suburb, where it now offers the lower wages typical of its new location. (1.) In this case some employees who previously commuted to the city from suburban residences will remain in their suburban homes and enjoy a welfare increase in terms of reduced commuting, but a loss in terms of reduced wages. (2.) Some workers who live in the city will, because of ties to both their residences and their jobs, begin to reverse commute. These workers will suffer a reduction in their welfare from both greater commuting costs and lower wages. These are real losses that must be counted in the full reckoning. (3.) Some workers will move residences from city to suburbs—these are taken to be "marginal" workers. At least as a first approximation, we assume that they maintain their same basic level of welfare under the new location as they had before. In particular, this means that any changes in their wages, land costs, amenities, and tax burden net out to a zero effect on their welfare. (4.) In addition to the three categories above, there may be some personnel changes in the firm's workforce. Of chief concern here is the situation in which a given job is held by a low-skilled worker, the primary wage earner of a low-income household, but after the move is held by a low-skilled worker from a medium- or high-income household. Here we assume that the low-income household in the city loses half the value of its former wages (although some may be made up by transfers from society at large.) The suburban household we assume had alternative activities of about equal value, so they experience little or no gain in welfare from taking on this job.

In short, our major theoretical starting points for evaluating the costs and benefits associated with a firm's intrametropolitan location decision are as follows:

1. Market prices of employed labor and land can be taken as fixed regardless of the firm's location choice. However, the firm's choice can result in the employment of otherwise involuntarily unemployed or underemployed resources.
2. In particular, the substitution of secondary and tertiary low-skilled suburban workers for primary low-skilled city workers results in a welfare loss for the latter without a corresponding welfare gain for the former.
3. Increases in externalities will be absorbed by the large majority of intramarginal households without leading to adjustments in their location.
4. Marginal households "moving" from city to suburb maintain roughly the same welfare and hence may impose fiscal losses on the city without achieving gains for themselves.
5. Heavily "entangled" households will face changes in commuting costs and wages.

NOTES

Chapter 1

1. For an extended discussion of how central business districts were revived, see Frieden and Sagalyn (1989).
2. Admittedly, poverty rates remain much lower in suburbs than in central cities. But despite the rapid flight of the affluent to distant suburbs, the large absolute growth of suburban poverty has increased the share of the suburban poor in the total suburban population from 7.9% in 1980 to 8.1% in 1990.

Chapter 2

1. More formally, we might say that both sides subscribe to the normative principles of applied welfare economics. This approach measures efficiency by summing up the dollar values of benefits and costs accruing to individuals. These calculations are then considered in conjunction with their distributional implications. While it is difficult to define the "best" distribution, there is broad agreement that other things unchanged (e.g., if efficiency is unaffected), a more equitable distribution is preferable to a less equitable one. Where significant gains can be made in efficiency and/or equity, some form of government intervention becomes warranted. Although widely used by liberal economists in the United States, this approach to welfare analysis can be contrasted with any number of alternatives; see note 48 below.
2. However, our approach does draw at several critical points on elements of the location theory of urban economics. These theoretical constructs will be introduced into the argument as needed. A theoretically inclined reader may at this point wish to consult appendix A3 for a quick introduction to the important propositions used to justify our empirical analysis.
3. We define low- and moderate-income households as those with total earnings in 1989 less than $30,000, middle-income households as those with total earnings between $30,000 and $75,000, and high-income households as those with more than $75,000.
4. For details of this calculation, see the discussion in appendix A1.1.
5. For details on the theoretical structure of the REMI model, see Treyz (1993). The model actually predicts a somewhat higher regional mul-

tiplier for an outer suburban siting and a somewhat smaller one for
central city siting. These differences are difficult to rationalize. Therefore we rescaled the REMI results to force equality between the two
multipliers. For the detailed industry breakdowns, see appendix A1.2.

6. We estimate that when the electrical equipment plant is located in the
city proper, about half of all new workers (direct, indirect, and induced)
live in the suburbs. This figure can be compared to the 37% (figure 1–
1) for the direct manufacturing workers alone. Less dramatically, the
placement of the plant in the outer suburbs leads to 15% of direct and
induced jobs going to central city residents, as opposed to only 7% for
the initial jobs alone. See appendixes A1.1 and A1.2 for the details of
these calculations.

7. We estimate that when the plant is placed in the outer suburbs, the total
of 2,400 jobs (1,000 for the original workers and 1,400 indirect and
induced) gives rise to about 1,240 new households (including direct,
indirect, and induced workers) spread about the region, but heavily
concentrated in the outer suburbs. An initial plant site in the central city
results in 103 more households, or a total of 1,345. Of this difference the
bulk, 99 households, have low or moderate incomes. See appendix A1.2
for details.

8. The major price of this detail is that the PUMS withholds addresses
and limits geographic identification to relatively large areas. These
disclosure constraints dictate the highly aggregate geography of the
present study, that is, central city, inner suburbs, and outer suburbs.

9. In several of our calculations, we expand the range of worker characteristics further to include information on a worker's individual income
as well as his or her household's income. For example, already in
estimating the number of new households we took into consideration
the ratio of individual income to household income.

10. Still, one might expect that the employment of supplementary workers
increases suburban vehicle ownership of their households. According
to the PUMS data, while this is true, the magnitude of the increase is
minimal.

11. Mark Hanson (1992) includes in his figure the costs of all automobile
accident-related personal injuries on the grounds that these are essentially subsidized through standard health insurance. These are not
formally externalities; Hanson calls them indirect subsidies. On the
other hand, his figure makes no allowance for pain and suffering or
death. DeLuchi's (OTA, 1994) estimate somewhat arbitrarily assumes
that the costs of accidents are divided equally between drivers responsible for accidents and the rest of the population. But these other drivers
and passengers in a sense "accept" the risk of accidents as a cost of the
convenience of driving.

12. In making this estimate, we relate land absorption to type of activity.
Informal discussions with planners in the area suggest that on the
average, in the outer suburbs, manufacturing absorbs 0.05 acres per
worker, transportation and public utilities 0.1 acre, and retailing and
wholesaling 0.2 acre; FIRE, services, and government each absorb 0.02
acres per worker. Construction absorbs no land per worker.

13. By assumption, abandonment is not a problem in the outer suburbs. Presumably low-income households there handle their housing problems as best they can, but their housing choices impose few if any externalities on their neighbors.

14. $75,000 = $1000*(0.27 abandoned units per poverty household*277 poverty households)
$29,000 = $1000*(0.27 abandoned units per poverty household*107 poverty households)

15. In the worst case, they can find alternative employment in other metropolitan areas.

16. In view of the considerable uncertainty of this figure, we conduct a sensitivity analysis below.

17. At this juncture one might reasonably ask why low-skilled city workers do not compete for suburban jobs or move to suburban residences. This is a central question of the mismatch literature. For many, the barrier is racial discrimination in housing and job markets. For a full discussion, consult the references cited above.

18. Our definition of low wage is $8 per hour in 1989 dollars. At this wage, a full-time worker putting in 50 weeks per year would earn $16,000 a year, a figure that would leave a family of 4 in poverty.

19. Since the magnitude of the mismatch externality is both large and relatively uncertain, it seems prudent to suggest a plausible range for this figure. The fundamental difficulty here derives from our paucity of knowledge concerning the opportunity cost experienced by low-wage workers. If we assert that low-wage/low-income workers have virtually no alternative opportunities, then the mismatch cost rises to $911,000 per year. If instead, we maintain the 50% figure from the text, but hold that low-wage workers from more affluent households have opportunity costs less than 100%, say 75%, then the mismatch cost falls to $228,000 per year.

20. As suggested, we assume that households, frustrated by the city's labor market, will move out of the Chicago metropolitan area. In fact, some, many or all of the unplaced low-income households will remain unemployed or underemployed in Chicago and its suburbs. Since their prospects are poor in other metropolitan areas, they have relatively little incentive to outmigrate. Whatever gains this implies for the rest of the nation are just offset by additional costs in the Chicago area.

21. In addition to the two groups identified in the text, there is a group of households representing net migrants (in or out of the metropolitan area) for each household type. For the changes in public costs associated with these households, see our discussion of "the rest of the nation" below.

22. For a more extensive discussion of the theoretical foundation of this claim, see appendix A3.

23. 16% versus 11%.

24. See below for a discussion of these nonresidential expenditures. Note that if a household moves from city to suburb, our basic assumption of well-functioning land and housing markets implies that their dwelling will not be abandoned. Why, then, do property and other taxes fall?

Presumably, the adjustment is made in terms of the pace of new or replacement construction responding to the modest decline in demand without a fundamental change in land or housing prices. The city will have one less housing unit. Investors in housing capital can achieve market returns elsewhere and hence do not have to be considered in our analysis.

25. The exception are public welfare expenditures, which presumably would not rise with the addition of newly employed households. These are excluded from expenditure figures shown below.

26. Presumably, marginal costs in the inner suburbs form an intermediate case between the city and outer suburbs. Some of these municipalities are themselves losing population and can easily accommodate new households. Others are still growing and thus are hard-pressed to expand public capital and service systems. With some uncertainty, we estimate marginal expenditures in these suburbs as a whole to be 50% of average expenditures, except for education; the latter, as in the central city, we estimate at 75%.

27. We estimate that in both the central city and the outer suburbs, low- and moderate-income households (those with annual incomes below $30,000) generate per household revenues equal to only 80% of the middle-income figure; high-income households (with annual incomes above $75,000) generate 170% of that figure. These estimates are based on property tax payments paid by homeowners at each income level in the three geographic areas (PUMS).

28. From PUMS data on public school enrollments by income group, we know that city schools are much more heavily used by lower-income families than by higher-income families. In the city, a new low-income household adds 120% of average public school costs per household, a middle-income household adds 100%, and a high-income household adds only 40%.

29. The exception to this conclusion is the work of Henry Bain on Montgomery County, Maryland, discussed extensively in Altshuler and Gomez-Ibanez, 1993. Bain attributes the extra cost of highways to businesses rather than to residents as the bulk of the literature does.

30. We make the basic assumption that nonresidential revenues from property taxes, utilities, and fees are proportional to the nonresidential share of total assessed value as reported in the 1987 Census of Governments. This allows us to calculate a nonresidential revenue per dollar of nonresidential assessed value. This ratio is taken to apply to new businesses. At the margin, we assume that new employers will have the same average assessment-to-employee ratio as old employers for the three geographic areas. These data appear below. For details, see appendix A1.3.

31. We explicitly excluded highway expenditures from the measurement of local fiscal subsidy; thus we are not double counting by including highway expenditures here.

32. To estimate the tax avoided by homeowners of each type, we assumed a 5% return on the average value and then multiplied by the marginal tax rate appropriate for a household's income.

33. This basic framework was already adopted in our estimates of public costs. As noted there, a more complete theoretical motivation of this approach is presented in appendix A3.
34. We take these wages to be $10 per hour for the low-income group, $20 for the middle-income group, and $40 for the high-income group. Since our income categories are based on household income, we adjust these for the share a worker contributes to his or her household income.
35. Again, note that this transfer may involve capital being moved from housing activities to other investment opportunities.
36. The PUMS has information on an individual's 1989 annual earnings from salary and self-employment, as well as his or her usual hours per week in 1989 and weeks worked in 1989. The estimate used here for the wage is then

hourly wage = (salary + self employment)/(weeks * hours).

37. The actual equations are presented in appendix A1.
38. Suburban employers may hire more qualified labor for a given job, rather than actually pay a lower wage. To adjust for this possibility, we took the actual earnings by industry and sex for central city workers, and using the equations from appendix A1, we estimated the expected cost of the same workforce in the inner suburbs and outer suburbs. Within each industry, we also standardized the gender distribution of workers at all locations to the metropolitan-wide average gender distribution for that industry. This adjustment is necessary to control for any differences in productivity between men and women within an industry.
39. These land prices are based on *Olcott's Land Values Blue Book of Chicago and Suburbs* (1994) and informal consultations with regional planners.
40. Also note, again, that we do not include here land cost differences for residential sites, since these differences are also considered in the residential costs and benefits section.
41. Notice that the case of construction wages is different from that of the overall wage differential between city and outer suburbs. The latter is presumably a compensating differential representing real gains in quality of life. The former is likely the product of bilateral bargaining under differing union strengths and hence a case of pure transfer.
42. This basic conclusion is supported by a rough sensitivity test of our results. Using the upper bound for the mismatch externality suggested above in note 21, the overall net loss rises to about $530,000 per year. With the lower bound we estimate a modest net gain from the outer suburban site: about $150,000 per year.
43. There is another practical reason to address the distributional effects: winners are likely to be favorably disposed to deconcentration and thus to support it in the political arena, while losers are likely to find deconcentration unattractive and thus to oppose it. Assessing distributional impacts gives a key to understanding political coalitions.

Chapter 3

1. Note that the above argument in no way diminishes the case for transfers from richer to poorer households. That case depends on a range of ethical, economic, and political considerations that have little to do with the matter at hand. However, the argument made here does imply that in carrying out noncash transfers-in-kind, we do well to consider carefully the material composition of those transfers. In particular, we should not overestimate the value of environmental quality and other externalities to those in severe need of basics.

2. Any bias in this assumption is toward understating the costs to low-income households. Such households might be more likely to live in closer proximity to heavy traffic areas.

3. Of course, analysts working with alternative normative systems might reach different conclusions. For example, conservatives have increasingly emphasized the principles of procedural justice in evaluating policies. From this perspective, modest improvements in equity would not be considered sufficient justification for government to intervene to significantly restrict the use rights of private property. On the other hand, an analysis drawing on Rawlsian notions of justice would have little interest in our efforts to calculate net efficiency effects, and instead would focus only on the impact of deconcentration on the most disadvantaged members of the society. This approach would most likely give a much sharper endorsement of intervention.

Chapter 4

1. The basic simulations resulted in the business services facility generating a multiplier just a tad larger when located in the outer suburbs as compared to the central city. The difference is not significant and we have standardized the multiplier and industry distribution for an outer suburban facility to equal that of the central city.

2. Overall we estimate that the business service facility with its 1,000 workers will generate 776 new households if located in the central city and 717 if located in the outer suburbs.

BIBLIOGRAPHY

Abbott, Carl, Deborah Howe, and Sy Adler. "Afterword." In *Planning the Oregon Way: A Twenty-Year Evaluation*, 209–19. Corvallis: Oregon State University Press, 1994.

Altshuler, Alan, and Jose Gomez-Ibanez. *Regulation for Revenue*. Washington, D.C.: Brookings Institution and Lincoln Institute of Land Policy, 1993.

———. "The Price of Exactions." *Governing*, January 1994, 65.

American Planning Association. *Growing Smart Legislative Guidebook*. Chicago: American Planning Association, 1997.

Angell, Cynthia, and Charles A. Shorter. "Impact Fees: Private-Sector Participation in Infrastructure Financing." *Government Finance Review* 4, no. 5 (1988): 19–21.

Ashauer, David. *Economic Impact of Illinois Tollway Improvements on the Regional Economy*. Illinois State Toll Highway Authority, 1990.

Ashworth, Stephen. "Harnessing Land and Development Values for Public Benefit." Cambridge, Mass.: Lincoln Institute of Land Policy, 1996.

Ayres, B. Drummond, Jr. "San Diego Council Approves 'Model' Nature Habitat Plan." *New York Times*, March 20, 1997, A16.

Baker, Karen, Steven Hinze, and Nina Manzi. "Minnesota's Fiscal Disparities Program." Minnesota House of Representatives Research Department, St. Paul, 1991.

Barnes, William R., and Larry C. Ledebur. *The U.S. Common Market of Local Economic Regions*. Washington, D.C.: National League of Cities, 1994.

Beasley, Steven, William Workman, and Nancy Williams. "Estimating Amenity Values of Urban Fringe Farmland: A Contingent Valuation Approach: Note." *Growth and Change* 17 (1986): 70–78.

Bergstrom, John, B. Dillman, and John Stoll. "Public Environment Amenity Benefits of Private Land: The Case of Prime Agricultural Land." *Southern Journal of Agricultural Economics* 17 (1985): 139–49.

Blackley, Paul. "Spatial Mismatch in Urban Labor Markets: Evidence from Large U.S. Metropolitan Areas." *Social Science Quarterly* 71 (1990): 39–52.

Boardman Anthony, David Greenberg, Aidan Vinin, and David Weimer. *Cost-Benefit Analysis: Concepts and Practice*. Upper Saddle River, N.J.: Prentice-Hall, 1996.

Burchell, Robert. *Impact Assessment of the New Jersey Interim State Development and Redevelopment Plan*. Trenton: New Jersey Office of State Planning, 1992.

Burchell, Robert, and David Listoskin. *Land, Infrastructure, Housing Costs and Fiscal Impacts Associated with Growth: The Literature on the Impacts of Sprawl versus Managed Growth*. Cambridge, Mass.: Lincoln Institute of Land Policy, 1995.

Burchell, Robert, David Listokin, and Arlene Pashman. *Regional Housing Opportunities for Lower Income Households: A Resource Guide to Affordable Housing and Regional Mobility Strategy*. New Brunswick, N.J.: Center for Urban Policy Research, Rutgers University, 1994.

Bureau of Economic Analysis. Regional Economic Information System CD-ROM. Washington, D.C.: U.S. Department of Commerce, Economics and Statistics Administration, Bureau of Economic Analysis, Regional Economic Measurement Division, 1993.

Cavalita, Nick. "Vale of Tiers." *Planning* 63, no. 3 (1997): 18–23.

Cervero, Robert. *American Suburban Centers: The Land Use-Transportation Link*. Boston: Unwin Hyman, 1989a.

———. "Jobs-Housing Balancing and Regional Mobility." *Journal of the American Planning Association* (1989b): 136–50.

Chernick, Howard, and Andrew Reschovsky. "Urban Fiscal Problems: Co-ordinating Actions Among Governments." Evanston, Ill.: Center for Urban Affairs and Policy Research, Northwestern University, 1994.

Chicago Department of Public Works. *Access to Jobs*. Chicago: Chicago Department of Public Works, 1990.

Cisneros, Henry G. *Regionalism: The New Geography of Opportunity*. Washington, D.C.: U.S. Department of Housing and Urban Development, 1995.

Clavel, Pierre, and Wim Wiewel. *Harold Washington and the Neighborhoods: Progressive City Government in Chicago, 1983–1987*. New Brunswick, N.J.: Rutgers University Press, 1991.

Cole, Sam. "A Community Accounting Matrix." *Economic Development Quarterly* 8 (1994): 107–26.

Connerly, Charles, E. "The Social Implications of Impact Fees." *Journal of American Planning Association* (Winter 1988): 75–78.

Cooper, Sandra. "Growth Control Evolves in Boulder." In *Growth Management Keeping on Target?* Edited by Douglas Porter. Washington, D.C.: Urban Land Institute, 1986.

Danish, Paul D. "Boulder's Self-Examination." In *Growth Management Keeping on Target?* Edited by Douglas Porter. Washington, D.C.: Urban Land Institute, 1986.

Deakin, Elizabeth. "Growth Controls and Growth Management: A Summary and Review of Empirical Research." In *Understanding Growth Management: Critical Issues and a Research Agenda*. Edited by David J. Brower, David R. Godschalk, and Douglas R. Porter, 3–21. Washington, D.C.: Urban Land Institute, 1989.

Decorla-Souza, Patrick, and Anthony Kane. "Peak Period Tolls: Precepts and Prospects." *Transportation* 19 (1992): 291–311.

Diamond, Peter, and Jerry Hausman. "Is Some Number Better than No Number?" *Journal of Economic Perspectives* 8 (1994): 45–64.

Dowall, David. *The Suburban Squeeze*. Berkeley: University of California Press, 1984.

Downs, Anthony. *Stuck in Traffic: Coping with Peak-Hour Traffic Congestion*. Washington, D.C.: Brookings Institution, 1992.

———. *New Visions of Metropolitan America*. Washington, D.C.: Brookings Institution and Lincoln Institute of Land Policy, 1994.

Dubin, Robin. "Commuting Patterns and Firm Decentralization." *Land Economics* 67 (1991): 15–29.

Ewing, Reid H. *Transportation and Land Use Innovations: When You Can't Pave Your Way out of Congestion*. Chicago: American Planning Association, 1997.

Feder, Barnaby. "Sowing Preservation: Towns are Slowing Invasion of Farms by Bulldozers." *New York Times*, March 20, 1997, C1.

Fischel, William A. "Comment on Carl Abbott's 'The Portland Region: Where City and Suburbs Talk to Each Other—and Often Agree.'" *Housing Policy Debate* 8, no. 1 (1997): 65–73.

Fischer, Paul B. "Comments." In *Affordable Housing and Public Policy: Strategies for Metropolitan Chicago*. Edited by Lawrence B. Joseph, 259–62. Chicago: Center for Urban Research and Policy Studies, University of Chicago, 1993.

Follain, James R., and Stephen Malpezzi. *Dissecting Housing Value and Rent: Estimates of Hedonic Indexes for Thirty-Nine Large SMSAs*. Washington, D.C.: Urban Institute, 1980.

Foster, Kathryn A. *The Political Economy of Special-Purpose Government*. Washington, D.C.: Georgetown University Press, 1997.

Frank, James E., Paul B. Downing, and Elizabeth R. Lines. "A National Survey of Sewer Impact Fees." *Journal of the Water Pollution Control Federation* 57, no. 11 (1985): 1055–61.

Franzen, Gail. Statement on "Chicago Tonight." Channel 11, WBEZ, November 21, 1996.

Frey, William, and Elaine Fielding. "Changing Urban Populations: Regional Restructuring, Racial Polarization and Poverty Concentration." *Cityscape* 1 (1995): 1–66.

Frieden, Bernard J., and Lynne Sagalyn. *Downtown, Inc: How America Rebuilds Cities*. Cambridge, Mass.: MIT Press, 1989.

Garreau, Joel. *Edge City: Life on the New Frontier*. New York: Doubleday, 1991.

Gleeson, Michael E. "The Effects of an Urban Growth Management System on Land Values." *Land Economics* 55, no. 3 (1979): 350–65.

Goodchild, Barry, Christine Booth, and John Henneberry. "Impact Fees: A Review of Alternatives and their Implications for Planning Practice in Britain." *The Town Planning Review* 67, no. 2 (1996): 161.

Gurwitt, Rob. "Saving the Aging Suburb." *Governing*, May 1993, 36–42.

Halstead, John. "Measuring the Non-market Value of Massachusetts Agricultural Land: A Case Study." *Journal of Northeastern Agricultural Economics Council* 13 (1984): 12–19.

Hanemann, Michael. "Valuing the Environment through Contingent Valuation." *Journal of Economic Perspectives* 8 (1994): 19–43.

Hanson, Mark E. "Automobiles Subsidies and Land Use: Estimates and Policy Responses." *Journal of the American Planning Association* 58, no. 1 (1992): 60–71.

Hill, Edward, H. Wolman, and C. C. Ford. "Can Suburbs Survive Without their Central Cities? Examining the Suburban Dependence Hypothesis." *Urban Affairs Review* 31, no. 12 (1995): 147–74.

Holzer, Harry, Keith Ihlanfeldt, and David Sjoquist. "Work, Search and Travel Among White and Black Youth." *Journal of Urban Economics* 35 (1994): 320–45.

Hughes, Mark Alan, with Julie E. Sternberg. *The New Metropolitan Reality: Where the Rubber Meets the Road in Antipoverty Policy.* Washington, D.C.: Urban Institute, 1992.

Ihlanfeldt, Keith R., and Jorge Martinez-Vazquez. "Alternative Value Estimates of Owner-Occupied Housing: Evidence on Sample Selection Bias and Systematic Errors." *Journal of Urban Economics* 20 (1986): 356–69.

Ihlanfeldt, Keith R., and David L. Sjoquist. "Job Accessibility and Racial Differences in Youth Employment Rates." *American Economic Review* 80 (1990): 267–76.

Jargowsky, Paul A. *Poverty and Place: Ghettos, Barrios, and the American City.* New York: Russell Sage Foundation, 1997.

Johnson, Gary T. "Impact Fees for Off-Site Road Improvements: Guidelines for Evaluating the Practicality of the Approach and for Designing Local Programs." *Transportation Research*, July 1990, 277–82.

Kain, John. "Housing Segregation, Negro Employment and Metropolitan Decentralization." *Quarterly Journal of Economics* 82 (1968): 175–97.

Kain, John, and Joseph Persky. "Alternatives to the 'Gilded Ghetto.'" *The Public Interest* 14 (1969): 77–91.

Kasarda, John. "Jobs, Migration, and Emerging Urban Mismatches." In *Urban Change and Poverty.* Edited by Michael McGreary and Laurence Lynn Jr. Washington, D.C.: National Academy Press, 1988.

———. "City Jobs and Residents on a Collision Course: The Urban Underclass Dilemma." *Economic Development Quarterly* 4 (1990): 313–19.

Keeler, Theodore E., and Kenneth A. Small. "Optimal Peak-Load Pricing, Investment and Service Levels on Urban Expressways." *Journal of Political Economy* 85 (1977): 1–25.

Kelly, Eric Damien. *Managing Community Growth: Policies, Techniques, and Impacts.* Westport, Conn.: Praeger Publishers, 1993.

Ladd, Helen. "Population Growth, Density, and the Costs of Providing Public Services." *Urban Studies* 29 (1992): 273–96.

Ladd, Helen F., and John Yinger. *America's Ailing Cities: Fiscal Health and the Design of Urban Policy*. Baltimore: Johns Hopkins University Press, 1991.

Lamar, Martha, et al. "Affordable Housing in New Jersey: The Results of Mount Laurel II and the Fair Housing Act." *Rutgers Law Review* 4 (1989): 1197–1214.

Lang, Robert E., and Steven P. Hornburg. "Planning Portland Style: Pitfalls and Possibilities." *Housing Policy Debate* 8, no. 1 (1997): 1–10.

Lemann, Nicholas. "The Myth of Community Development." *New York Times Magazine*, January 9, 1994, 27.

Levine, Jonathan C. "Equity in Infrastructure Finance: When are Impact Fees Justified?" *Land Economics* 70, no. 2 (1994): 210–22.

Levitan, Sar A. *Programs in Aid of the Poor*. 6th ed. Baltimore: Johns Hopkins University Press, 1990.

Liu, Nan. *Urban Highway Congestion: An Economic Analysis of Second-Best Congestion Pricing Schemes*, Ph.D. dissertation, University of Illinois at Chicago, 1995.

Lopez, Rigoberto, Farhed Shah, and Marilyn Attolbello. "Amenity Benefits and the Optimal Allocation of Land." *Land Economics* 70, no. 1 (1994): 53–62.

MacKenzie, James, Roger Dower, and Donald Chen. *The Going Rate: What it Really Costs to Drive*. World Resources Institute, 1992.

Madden, Janice. "Why Women Work Closer to Home." *Urban Studies* 18 (1981): 181–94.

Martin, Judith. Statement at The Metropolis Project Fall Seminar, Cantigny, Ill., October 27, 1995, n.p.

Massey, Douglas S., and Nancy A. Denton. *American Apartheid: Segregation and the Making of the American Underclass*. Cambridge, Mass.: Harvard University Press, 1993.

Mattoon, Rick. "Can Alternative Forms of Governance Help Metropolitan Areas?" *Economic Perspectives* 19, no. 6 (1995): 20–32.

McGuire, Therese. "The Effect of New Firm Locations on Local Property Taxes." *Journal of Urban Economics* 22 (1987): 223–29.

Mead, Timothy D. "Who Killed Cock Robin? The failure of metropolitan reform in Charlotte–Mecklenburg." Presented at the Urban Affairs Association Conference, April 1997.

Metropolitan Planning Council. "Creating a Regional Community: The Case for Cooperation." Chicago: Metropolitan Planning Council, 1995.

Mills, Edwin. *Studies in the Structure of the Urban Economy*. Baltimore: Johns Hopkins University Press, 1972.

Mills, Edwin, and Bruce Hamilton. *Urban Economics*. 4th ed. Glenview, Ill.: Scott, Foresman, 1989.

Mohring, Herbert, and David Anderson. "Congestion Pricing for the Twin Cities Metropolitan Area." Minneapolis: CURA Resource Collection, Center for Urban and Regional Affairs, University of Minnesota, 1994.

Morris, Marya. "Taking the Bite Out of Big Projects." *Planning* 63, no. 2 (1997): 20–24.

Morrison, S. A. "A Survey of Road Pricing." (1986): 87–97.

National Congress for Community Economic Development. *Against All Odds: The Achievements of Community-Based Development Organizations.* Washington, D.C.: National Congress for Community Economic Development, 1989.

National Safety Council. *Accident Facts.* Chicago: National Safety Council, 1990.

Navarro, Mireya. "Rich Areas in Miami Talk Secession." *New York Times,* November 16, 1996, A8.

Nelson, Arthur C. "Development Impact Fees." *Journal of the American Planning Association* (Winter 1988): 3–6.

Nelson, Arthur C., and James B. Duncan. *Growth Management Principles and Practices.* Chicago: Planners Press, American Planning Association, 1995.

Nelson, Arthur C., James E. Frank, and James C. Nicholas. "Positive Influence of Impact-Fee in Urban Planning and Development." *Journal of Urban Planning and Development* 118 (1992): 59–64.

Nelson, Arthur C., James C. Nicholas, and Julian C. Jurgensmeyer. "Critical Elements of Development Impact-Fee Programs." *Journal of Urban Planning and Development* 116, no. 1 (1990): 34–47.

Oakland, William, and William Testa. "Does Business Development Raise Taxes: An Empirical Appraisal." *Economic Perspectives* 19 (1995): 22–32.

OECD/ECMT Organization for Economic Co-Operation and Development/European Conference of Ministers of Transportation. *Urban Travel and Sustainable Development.* Paris: OECD, 1995.

Olcott's Land Values Blue Book of Chicago and Suburbs. Park Ridge, Ill.: George C. Olcott and Company, 1994.

Orfield, Myron. *Metropolitics: A Regional Agenda for Community and Stability.* Washington, D.C.: Brookings Institution and Lincoln Institute of Land Policy, 1997.

OTA, U.S. Congress, Office of Technology Assessment. *The Technological Reshaping of Metropolitan America.* OTA-ETI-643. Washington, D.C.: U.S. Government Printing Office, 1995.

Parzen, Julia. "Innovations in Metropolitan Cooperation." In *The Metropolitan Initiative: Briefing Book for the Chicago Regional Forum.* Chicago: Center for Neighborhood Technology, 1997.

Persky, Joseph, Elliott Sclar, and Wim Wiewel. *Does America Need Cities: An Urban Investment Strategy for National Prosperity.* Washington, D.C.: United States Conference of Mayors and Economic Policy Institute, 1992.

Porter, Douglas R. "Will Developers Pay to Play?" *Journal of the American Planning Association* 54, no. 1 (1988): 59–64.

———. *Managing Growth in America's Communities.* Washington, D.C.: Island Press, 1997.

Portney, Paul R. "The Contingent Valuation Debate: Why Economists Should Care." *Journal of Economic Perspectives* 8 (1994): 3–17.

Pozdena, Randall. "Unlocking Gridlock." *Federal Reserve Bank of San Francisco Weekly Letter*, December 1988, 1–5

President's Council on Sustainable Development. *Building on Consensus: A Progress Report on Sustainable America*. Washington, D.C., January 1997.

Public Private Transportation Network (PPTN). *Accel Transportation: Anatomy of a Reverse-Commute Service*. Washington, D.C.: Public Private Transportation Network, n.d.

Quercia, Roberto G., and George C. Galster. "Threshold Effects and the Expected Benefits of Attracting Middle-Income Households to the Central City." *Housing Policy Debate* 8, no. 2 (1997): 409–36.

Real Estate Research Corporation. *The Costs of Sprawl: Environmental and Economic Costs of Alternative Residential Development Patterns at the Urban Fringe*. Washington, D.C.: U.S. Government Printing Office, 1974.

Rosenbaum, James, E. "Closing the Gap: Does Residential Integration Improve the Employment and Education of Low-Income Blacks?" In *Affordable Housing and Public Policy: Strategies for Metropolitan Chicago*. Edited by Lawrence B. Joseph, 233–57. Chicago: Center for Urban Research and Policy Studies, University of Chicago, 1993.

Rosentraub, Mark S., and Sam Nunn. *City and Suburb: Linkages, Benefits, and Shared Responsibilities*. Indianapolis: Center for Urban Policy and the Environment, Indiana University, 1994.

Rosentraub, Mark S., Samuel Nunn, Drew Klacik, Michael Przybylski, and Joseph Rubleske. *Building the Economic Future of Metropolitan Indianapolis: A Proposal for Regional Cooperation and Finance*. Indianapolis: Center for Urban Policy and the Environment, Indiana University, 1996.

Ross, Dennis H., and Scott Ian Thorpe. "Impact Fees: Practical Guide for Calculation and Implementation." *Journal of Urban Planning and Development* 118, no. 3 (1992): 106–18.

Rusk, David. *Cities Without Suburbs*. Washington, D.C.: The Woodrow Wilson Center Press, 1993.

Savitch, Hank V. "The Ties that Bind: Central Cities, Suburbs, and the New Metropolitan Region." *Economic Development Quarterly* 7, no. 4 (1993): 341–57.

Savitch, Hank V., and Ronald K. Vogel. *Regional Politics: America in a Post-City Age*. Thousand Oaks, Calif.: Sage, 1996.

Schill, Michael H. "Deconcentrating the Inner City Poor." *Chicago Kent Law Review*. 67: 795–853.

Siegel, Wendy, and Maryann Mason. *The Power to Shape the Future: An Analysis of Decision Making in the Regional Transportation Planning Process and Impacts on the Urban Poor*. Chicago: Chicago Institute on Urban Poverty and Heartland Alliance for Human Needs and Human Rights, 1995.

Siemon, Charles. "Who Bears the Cost." *Law and Contemporary Problems* 50 (1987): 115–26.

Singell, Larry D., and Jane H. Lillydahl. "An Empirical Examination of the Effect of Impact Fees on the Housing Market." *Land Economics* 66, no. 1 (1990): 82–92.

Skidmore, Mark, and Michael Peddle. "Do Development Impact Fees Reduce the Rate of Residential Development?" *Growth & Change* 29, no. 4 (1998): 383–400.

Small, Kenneth A. "The Incidence of Congestion Tolls on Urban Highways." *Journal of Urban Economics* 13 (1983): 90–111.

Small, Kenneth A., Clifford Winston, and Carol A. Evans. *Road Work: A New Highway Pricing and Investment Policy*. Washington, D.C.: Brookings Institution, 1989.

Stanback, Thomas M. *The New Suburbanization: Challenge to the Central City*. Boulder: Westview Press, 1991.

Stroud, Nancy. "Legal Considerations of Development Impact Fees." *Journal of the American Planning Association* 54, no. 1 (1988): 29–37.

Swindell, David W., and Roger Parks. "Neighborhoods and Unigov." In *The Hudnut Years in Indianapolis, 1976–1991*. Edited by William H. Hudnut III, 153–63. Bloomington: University of Indiana Press, 1995.

Tindale, Steven A. "Impact Fees-Issues, Concepts, and Approaches." *ITE Journal* 61, no. 5 (1991): 33–39.

Treyz, George. *Regional Economic Modeling: A Systematic Approach to Economic Forecasting and Policy Analysis*. Boston: Kluwer Academic Publishers, 1993.

Turner, Margery Austin. "Achieving a New Urban Diversity: What Have We Learned?" *Housing Policy Debate* 8, no. 2 (1997): 295–305.

U.S. Bureau of the Census. *Census of Population and Housing, 1990: Public Use Microdata Sample U.S. Technical Documentation*. Washington, D.C.: The Bureau of the Census, 1992.

U.S. Congress, Office of Technology Assessment. *Saving Energy in U.S. Transportation*. OTA-ETI-589. Washington, D.C.: U.S. Government Printing Office, 1994.

Urban Institute. *The Costs of Highway Crashes*. Prepared by the Urban Institute for the U.S. Federal Highway Administration, FWHA-RD-91-055, Technical Summary, Washington, D.C., June 1991.

Vidal, Avis. *Rebuilding Communities: A National Study of Urban Community Development Corporations*. New York: Community Development Research Center, New School for Social Research, 1992.

Vogel, Ronald K. "Metropolitan Government." In *Handbook of Research on Urban Politics and Policy in the United States*. Edited by Ronald K. Vogel, 185–96. Westport, Conn.: Greenwood Press, 1997.

Voith, Richard. "City and Suburban Growth: Substitutes or Complements." *Business Review*, September/October 1992, pp. 21ff.

———. "The Tax Treatment of Housing: Its Effects on Bounded and Unbounded Communities." Working Paper no. 98-23. Philadelphia: Economic Research Division, Federal Reserve Bank of Philadelphia, 1998.

Wheaton, William C. "Income and Urban Residence: An Analysis of Consumer Demand for Location." *American Economic Review* 67, no. 4 (1977): 620–31.

White, Michelle. "Firm Suburbanization and Urban Subcenters." *Journal of Urban Economics* 3 (1976): 323–43.

Wiewel, Wim, and Joseph Persky. "Urban Productivity and the Neighborhoods: The Case for a Federal Neighborhood Strategy." *Environment and Planning C: Government and Policy* 12 (1994): 473–83.

Williams, Kristine M. (1991). "Managing Developments of Regional Impact." *Planning and Zoning News*. October, 1991. pp. 5–9.

Wilson, William J. *The Truly Disadvantaged: The Inner City, the Underclass, and Public Policy*. Chicago: University of Chicago Press, 1987.

———. *Poverty, Joblessness, and Family Structure in the Inner City: A Comparative Perspective*. Paper prepared for presentation at the Chicago Urban Poverty and Family Life Conference sponsored by the Irving B. Harris Graduate School of Public Policy Studies at the University of Chicago and the Social Science Research Council of New York, 1991.

———. *When Work Disappears: The World of the New Urban Poor*. New York: Vintage Books, 1997.

Wolman, Harold, Coit Cook Ford III, and Edward Hill. (1994) "Evaluating the Success of Urban Success Stories." *Urban Studies* 31, no. 6: 835–50.

Wright, Patricia. The Plan to Voucher Out Public Housing: An analysis of the Chicago experience and a case study of the proposal to redevelop the Cabrini–Green housing area. Chicago: Nathalie P. Voorhees Center, University of Illinois at Chicago, 1997.

INDEX

Abandonment. *See* Housing abandonment

ACCEL, 114, 115

Affordable suburban housing. *See* Suburban housing programs

African Americans: housing programs, 118; increasing poverty, 125; reduced job opportunities for men, 125; wage costs, 68

Agglomeration economies, 129, 159

Air pollution: calculation of, 139; costs, 34, 40–41; distribution of costs, 76; in inner suburbs, 153, 156

Allegheny County Regional Asset District, 123

Altobello, Marilyn, 44

Altshuler, Alan, 103

American Law Institute, 107

American Planning Association, land use planning guidebook, 107

Anchorage–Anchorage Borough, 127

Anderson, David, 38

Annexation, 127, 128–29

Annual permits, 109

Applied welfare economics, 87, 163 n.3

Automobile accidents. *See* Traffic accidents

Automobile registration fees, 102

Auto-related externalities, calculation of distribution, 149–50

Bain, Henry, 166 n.31

Balanced development, 108

Bergen, 102

Bid-rent function, 159

Blacks. *See* African Americans

Boston, 109

Boulder, Colorado, 109, 110

Bridges to Work Program, 114, 115

Brownfield development. *See* Central cities; Central city manufacturing facilities

Buffalo, 16

Business services deconcentration: business services workers, 89–91; calculation of gains and losses, 147–49; distribution of costs and benefits by income and residence, 95–97; externalities associated with, 91–92; in inner suburbs, 156–58; private costs and benefits, 69–71, 93–94; public-sector costs, 93; total costs and benefits, 94

Business taxes, 70–71; savings in inner suburbs, 154–55

Calculations, 135–51

Cape Cod Commission, 107

Capital income, distribution of by income level, 84–85

Car pooling, 36, 101

Census of Governments, 54

Central cities: business district recovery, 15–16; construction costs in, 71; declining and growing, 13; deconcentration,

179

Central cities: (*cont.*)
14–18; housing abandonment,
45–47; land costs, 70; lower
marginal expenditures relative
to suburbs, 55; redevelopment,
45, 50–51, 125–26, 132
Central city manufacturing
facilities: air pollution costs,
41; annual accident costs, 40;
generation of less congestion
versus suburban plants, 36–37;
land use, 42–43; local fiscal
impact, 59; lower-income
workers in, 28, 48; lower
private benefits than suburban
plants, 64–66; lower residential
fiscal impact than suburban
plants, 57–58; nonresidential
property assessments per
employee, 58; and number
of households not in poverty,
46; number of housing
abandonments, 46; number of
new households generated, 31;
suburban commuters to, 27
Central city workforce: commuting,
27, 36; low-income workers,
28, 47–48; use of public
transportation, 34
Charlotte–Mecklenburg County,
128
Chen, Donald, 39–40, 41, 61
Chicago: costs of commuting,
38–39, 74; determinants of
wages for men and women,
148; Gautreaux program, 118,
120; growth of outer suburbs,
18, 19; impact fees, 55; inner
suburbs, 21; Leadership
Council for Metropolitan
Open Communities, 118;
LeClaire Court Resident
Management Association, 114,
115; redevelopment programs,
124; reverse commuting
programs, 114; Suburban Job

Link, 114; transit system, 114;
value of land, 44
Chicago Transit Authority, 123
Child care, 67
Cincinnati, 109
City-county consolidation, 127–28
Cleveland: deconcentration, 14;
growth of outer suburbs, 18, 19
Committed (residentially) workers:
commuting time, 64–65,
145–46, 161, 162; losses in
wages, 65–66, 161, 162
Community Development Block
Grant program, 124
Commuting, 33; by central city
workforce, 27, 36; commuting
times, 36, 67, 159; costs of in
Chicago, 38–39, 74; by outer
suburban workforce, 36, 75;
by residentially committed
workers, 64–65, 145–46, 161,
162; by suburban residents
to central city jobs, 16, 35;
value of commuting time, 65;
value of commuting time to
women, 67–68; by worker
types, 37
Competitiveness, policies that
enhance: attracting growth to
older areas, 124–25; regional
governance, 126–30
Concurrency planning, 109, 112
Congestion. *See* Traffic congestion
Congestion pricing. *See* Traffic
congestion pricing
Congestion Pricing Pilot Program,
102
Connerly, Charles E., 105
Construction costs: calculation of,
149; distribution of by income
levels, 85; in suburbs versus
central city, 71
Consumption patterns, 160
Contingent evaluation methods, 44
Cook County, 152
Cost-benefit analysis, 25, 44, 74

Dayton, Ohio, 121
Deconcentration, metropolitan.
    See Business services
    deconcentration; Employment
    deconcentration; Manufactur-
    ing deconcentration
Decorla-Souza, Patrick, 38
DeLuchi, 40, 41, 61, 164 n.13
Denton, Nancy A., 125
Denver, Scientific and Cultural
    Facilities District, 123
Design standards, 110
Detroit, growth of outer suburbs,
    18, 19
Development rights, 43
Developments of Regional Impacts
    (DRI), Florida, 107
Discrimination: against central city
    residents in suburban jobs, 65,
    165 n.19; housing, 116, 125
Distribution of costs and benefits
    of deconcentration: calculation
    of, 149–51; for inner suburban
    business services, 158; for
    inner suburban manufacturing,
    155–56; for outer suburban
    business services, 95–97; for
    outer suburban manufacturing,
    73–87
*Does America Need Cities? An Urban
    Investment Strategy for National
    Prosperity* (Persky), 132
Dower, Roger, 39–40, 41, 61
Downs, Anthony, 102
Downtown revitalization, 15–16,
    125
Dubin, Robin, 68
Duncan, James B., 112
Dupage County, Illinois, impact
    fees, 106–7

Economic redevelopment, 45,
    50–51, 124–26, 132
Edge cities, 15–16, 18, 89
Education, public, higher use of by
    low-income households, 56,
    166 n.29
Educational investment, 132
Educational level, and place-
    of-work effects on wages,
    68
Electrical equipment industry, 25
Electronic credit cards, 102
Employment deconcentration:
    defined, 12–14; effect of
    suburban housing programs
    on costs and benefits of, 120;
    effects on public finance,
    17; impact on efficiency,
    16–17; inequitable, 22;
    and inner suburbs, 20–22;
    laissez-faire argument for,
    160; magnification of spillover
    effects of sprawl, 17; and
    outer suburbs, 18–20; policies,
    comparison of, 131–33; policies
    that constrain, 101–13; policies
    that enhance competitiveness,
    124–26, 132; policies that
    redistribute benefits of growth,
    113–24; private gains, 17;
    and slower growth, 14. *See
    also* Business services decon-
    centration; Manufacturing
    deconcentration
Empowerment Zone and
    Enterprising Communities
    program, 124
Entangled households. *See*
    Committed (residentially)
    workers
Entrepreneurial Services Challenge,
    114
Environmentally sensitive areas,
    110
Evans, Carol A., 38
Exactions, 103, 106, 118
Exclusionary zoning, 121
Externalities, 162; associated
    with inner suburban versus
    central city business services,
    156–57; associated with
    inner suburban versus central

Externalities (*cont.*)
city manufacturing, 153–56;
associated with outer suburban
versus central city business
services, 91–92; associated
with outer suburban versus
central city manufacturing,
34–35, 49–51, 63, 78–79,
153–56; calculation of, 138–41;
calculation of distribution,
149–51; distribution
of for manufacturing
deconcentration, 73–80

Farmland: preferential tax
treatment, 43; preservation,
109; value of, 44
Federal transportation programs,
114, 115
Fiscal flight, 52
Florida, 107, 109

Gasoline taxes, 99
Gautreaux program, Chicago, 118,
120
Gomez-Ibanez, Jose, 103
Greater Portland Metropolitan
Service District, 128
Greater Vancouver Regional
District, 109
Greenbelts, 109
Greenfield development.
See Business services
deconcentration; Employment
deconcentration; Manufactur-
ing deconcentration
Growth management, 100, 108–10,
130–31; arguments for and
against, 111–12; defined,
108; effects of, 110–11;
requirements for successful
programs, 112–13

Hanson, Mark E., 40, 164 n.13
High-income households: defined,
163 n.5; generation of higher
external costs, 49; generation

of larger surpluses, 56; greater
benefits gained from business
services deconcentration,
95–96; and single-family
dwellings, 42
Highway construction, costs
associated with, 57
Highway subsidies, 60–61, 63, 166
n.33; average versus marginal
costs, 60–61; and business
services deconcentration, 93,
157; calculation of, 144; and
manufacturing deconcentration, 60–61, 63, 154
Hispanic workers, wage costs, 68
Home mortgage interest, 61–62,
93, 99, 144, 154, 157
Home production, 67
Hong Kong, 102
Housing abandonment: calculation
of, 140; calculation of
distribution, 150; distribution
of costs, 84; distribution of
costs by income, 77; external
effects of, 46; manufacturing
deconcentration and, 34,
45–47, 66–67; in outer suburbs,
164 n.15; relation to poverty,
45–46
Housing and Urban Development
(HUD), Department of, 114,
115; Moving to Opportunity
demonstration program, 119;
Section 8 Portability Policy
and Housing Assistance Plan,
117, 118
Housing certificate programs, 118
Housing discrimination, 116
Housing programs, suburban. *See*
Suburban housing programs
Housing subsidies: calculation
of, 144; and inner suburban
business services, 157; owner-
occupied, 61–62, 93, 99, 144,
154, 157
Human capital, differences in, 160

Ihlanfeldt, Keith R., 46
Impact fees, 19–20, 55, 100, 103–8, 112, 130, 132, 142; burden of, 104; calculation of, 105–6; effect on competitiveness, 106; regional, 107–8; and use controls, 105
Implicit earnings, 61
Implicit payments, 59
Inclusionary zoning, 119
Income: declining, in inner suburbs, 21; differences in commuting by, 36; distribution of deconcentration costs by, 76–82, 84, 85; and job location, 28–31; and residential distribution, 90–91. *See also* High-income households; Low-income households; Moderate-income households
Indirect jobs, 32–33
Indirect subsidies, 164 n.13
Induced jobs, 32–33, 91
Information-service economy, 16
Infrastructure reinvestment, 132
Inner suburbs: attracting growth to, 124; decline of manufacturing, 21; decline of real median income, 21; effects of employment deconcentration, 20–22; flight of retailers, 21; poverty, 21; problems similar to those of inner city, 152; provision of public services, 21–22
Inner suburbs, business services deconcentration to, 156–58; distribution, 158; externalities, 156–57; net effects, 158; private benefits, 157–58; public-sector costs, 157
Inner suburbs, manufacturing deconcentration to: accidents, 153; automobile-related congestion, 153; business tax savings, 154–55; distribution

of effects of, 155–56; highway subsidies, 154; labor mismatch, 153; land costs, 154–55; marginal costs, 166 n.28; net effects, 155; nonresidential revenues, 153; owner-occupied subsidies, 154; pollution externalities, 153; private benefits, 154–55; public-sector costs, 153–54; residential revenues, 153–54; wage savings, 154–55
Intergovernmental transfers, 57
Intermodal Surface Transportation Efficiency Act (ISTEA), 102, 113, 114

Jacksonville–Duval County, 127
Jargowsky, Paul A., 125
Job location, and household income, 28–31
Job sprawl. *See* Employment deconcentration

Kain, John, 23

Labor, opportunity cost of, 47
Land absorption: nonresidential, 164 n.14; residential, 139
Land costs: and business taxes, calculation of, 148–49; of deconcentration, 70, 159; in inner suburbs, 154–55
Land restrictions, 108
Land/structure owners, 66–67, 147
Land use planning, 105
Land values, 66
Leadership Council for Metropolitan Open Communities, Chicago, 118
LeClaire Court Resident Management Association, Chicago, 114, 115
Lemann, Nicholas, 125
Lexington–Fayette County, 127
Linkage fees, 118

Local fiscal impacts, of manufacturing deconcentration, 51–53; calculation of distribution, 151; distribution of costs by income group, 81–82; distribution of costs by location, 80–81; nonresidential impacts, 58–59, 63; per new household by income and location, 55–57; residential impacts, 54–58, 63; total, 59

Lopez, Rigoberto, 44

Los Angeles, 41, 124

Louisville, Kentucky, 121

Low-income households: commuter travel time, 36; defined, 163 n.5; net costs of, 56–57

Low-skilled workers, 28–29

MacKenzie, James, 39–40, 41, 61

Madden, Janice, 30

Manufacturing deconcentration: distribution of externalities, 74–79; distribution of private costs and benefits, 84–86; distribution of public subsidy costs, 80–83; externalities, 34–35, 50–51, 63, 153–56; externalities outside the region, 49–50, 78–79; and housing abandonment, 34, 45–47, 66–67; lack of efficiency gains over central city development, 22, 26–27; private benefits versus social costs of, 23–25, 63; private costs and benefits of, 64–72; and spatial mismatch of jobs, 47–48, 50–51; spread effects, 31–33; and traffic accidents, 34; and traffic congestion, 34, 35–39

Manufacturing workforce: by household income, 29; importance of residential location to, 30; lower income of in central cities, 28; residential patterns, 27–28

Marginal amenity benefit, 44

Marginal costs: highway subsidies, 60–61; in inner suburbs, 166 n.28

Marginal households, 161, 162

Marginal revenues, intergovernmental transfers as, 57

Market economy, planning in, 11–12

Market prices, fixed, 162

Marriage, wage costs of, 68

Martinez-Vazquez, Jorge, 46

Massachusetts, specialized access to appeal or reward in, 120

Massey, Douglas S., 125

Mass transit. See Public transit systems

Metropolitan deconcentration. See Business services deconcentration; Employment deconcentration; Manufacturing deconcentration

Metropolitan planning, 11–12

Metropolitan Sustainable Development Working Group, 133

Miami, 129

Microsimulation, 24, 25

Middle class, flight from cities, 16

Minneapolis, poverty in inner suburbs, 21

Minneapolis–St. Paul, tax-base sharing, 121–22, 131

Minorities, housing and job discrimination against, 116, 125, 165 n.19

Mobile households, 53, 65, 67

Model Cities, 124

Model Land Development Code, 107

Moderate-income households, defined, 163 n.5

Mohring, Herbert, 38

Monocentric model, 68

Montgomery County, Maryland, affordable housing strategies,

119, 131

Mortgage interest tax exemption, 61–62, 93, 99, 144, 154, 157

Motorists, privacy of, 102

Moving to Opportunity demonstration program, Department of Housing and Urban Development (HUD), 119

Multifamily dwellings: low-income households among, 42; rental units, 61

Multiplier effects: calculation of, 136–37; of inner suburban business services facilities, 157; of inner suburban manufacturing facilities, 153; of manufacturing deconcentration, 32–33

Multistakerholder processes, 109

Nashville–Davidson County, 127

National externalities: calculation of, 141; calculation of distribution, 150; distribution of by income, 78–79

National subsidies: calculation of distribution, 151; distribution of costs by income, 82

Neighborhood development programs, 124–26

Neighborhood economies, declining, 16

Neighborhood quality, value of, 46

Nelson, Arthur C., 112

New York City, redevelopment programs, 124

Nonresidential impacts: of business services deconcentration, 93, 95; land absorption, calculation of, 139; of manufacturing deconcentration, 58–59, 63

Nonresidential revenues, 166 n.32; calculation of, 143–44; and inner suburban manufacturing facilities, 153

Office building boom, 14–15

Office of Economic Opportunity, 124

Open planning processes, 104

Open space: calculation of distribution of costs, 150; calculation of loss, 139; cost of loss, 20, 34; distribution of costs across income levels and location, 76–77; and inner suburban business services facilities, 156; mechanisms for maintaining, 43; value of, 41–44, 66

Opportunity cost, of labor, 47–48

Oregon, growth management controls, 109, 110–11

Orfield, Myron, 122

Oslo, 102

Outer suburban manufacturing facilities: air pollution costs, 41; auto-related costs, 34, 40; capital costs of residential development, 55; construction costs, 71; externalities associated with, 34–35; and housing abandonments, 46; housing subsidies, 62; land appreciation, 66; land costs, 70; land use, 42; local fiscal impact, 59; marginal versus average costs, 54–55; net cost in neighborhood conditions, 46; number of new households generated, 31; out-of-region benefits, 49–50; overall costs and benefits, 72; private benefits, 64–66; public-sector costs, 63; resident costs, 64–66; taxes for public services, 51–52; wage loss to low-wage workers from low-income households, 48

Outer suburban workforce: automobile reliance, 34; commuting statistics, 36,

Outer suburban workforce: (*cont.*) 75; lower wage levels, 64; secondary wage earners among, 33, 48

Owner-occupied housing subsidies, 61–62, 93, 144, 154, 157

Parenthood, wage costs, 68

Parks, Roger, 42

Peak-hour road pricing. *See* Traffic congestion pricing

Philadelphia: inner suburbs, 21; population increase versus land area increase, 14

Phoenix, population increase versus land area increase, 13

Pittsburgh, 14

Pittsford, New York, 109

Place-of-work effects, on wages by educational level, 68

Police services, 61

Policies. *See* Employment deconcentration

Pollution. *See* Air pollution

Population caps, 109

Population deconcentration, 12–13

Portland, Oregon, growth management controls, 109, 110–11, 112

Portland Metropolitan Services District, 122–23

Poverty: in inner suburbs, 21; lack of effect of housing programs on, 120; rates of in suburbs relative to central cities, 163 n.2; relation to housing abandonment, 45–46; role of racial segregation in creating, 125

Pozdena, Randall, 38

President's Council on Sustainable Development, 133

Private costs and benefits: of business services deconcentration, 93–94; calculation of, 145–47; calculation of distribution, 151; of inner suburban business services facilities, 157–58; of inner suburban manufacturing facilities, 154–55; of manufacturing deconcentration, 64–72

Property taxes, 107, 166 n.28

Public schools, higher use of by low-income households, 56, 166 n.29

Public-sector costs: calculation of, 141–45; subsidies, calculation of distribution, 151

Public-sector costs, of business services deconcentration: distribution of, 93; to inner suburbs, 153–54

Public-sector costs, of manufacturing deconcentration, 51–63; distribution of, 80–83; highway subsidies, 60–61, 63; housing subsidies, 61–62; to inner suburbs, 153–54; local fiscal impacts, 51–53; measuring, 52–53; nonresidential impacts, 58–59, 63; outside the area, 62–63; residential impacts, 54–58; total, 63

Public services: cost of in central city versus outer suburbs, 57; decline of in inner suburbs, 21–22

Public transit systems: ridership, 101; in the suburbs, 35, 115

Public Use Microdata Sample (PUMS), 24, 27, 33, 135, 152

Racial discrimination, in jobs and housing, 116, 165 n.19

Racial segregation, role of in creating poverty neighborhoods, 125

Rational nexus test, 104

Reconcentration, 124–26

Redevelopment programs, 45, 50–51, 124–26, 132

Redistributive taxation, 52

Regional Economic Models Incorporated (REMI) model, 32, 33, 91, 136, 152, 163 n.7
Regional governance, 101, 126–30, 132
Regional impact fees, 107–8
Regional planning agencies, 113
Regional review, 109
Regional taxes, 127
Regional Transportation Authority (RTA), Chicago, 123
Rental subsidies, 118
Renters, 77
Resident benefits and costs: calculation of, 145–47; calculation of distribution, 151; distribution of by income level, 84; of manufacturing location, 64–66
Residential choices, 30, 161–62
Residential development impact fees, 104
Residential expansion: capital costs of, 55; land absorption, 42, 139
Residential impacts: of business services deconcentration, 93, 95; of manufacturing deconcentration, 54–58, 63
Residential location theory, 67
Residentially committed workers. See Committed (residentially) workers
Residential patterns, of manufacturing workforce, 27–28
Residential revenues: calculation of, 141–43; in inner suburbs, 153–54
Residential succession, 21
Retailers, decline of in inner suburbs, 21
Reverse commuting, 27, 58, 64, 65, 100, 113–16, 131, 132, 161
Ride-sharing, 36, 101
Road-building expenditures. See Highway subsidies

Rochester, New York, 121
Rusk, David, 128

St. Louis, population increase versus land area increase, 14
San Diego, California, land use plan, 109–10, 112
Scientific and Cultural Facilities District, Denver, 123
Seattle: effects of growth management, 110; greenbelt, 109
Secondary business activities, 42
Secondary workers. See Supplementary workers
Section 8 Portability Policy and Housing Assistance Plan, HUD, 117, 118
Shah, Farhed, 44
Sidewalks, 42
Singapore, 102
Single-family dwellings, 42, 61
Slow-growth advocacy, 104
Small, Kenneth A., 38, 101, 102
Social costs: of manufacturing deconcentration, 23–25, 63; of traffic accidents, 39–40; traffic congestion, 38–39
Spatial mismatch of jobs: and business services deconcentration, 92; calculation of, 140–41; calculation of distribution, 150; distribution of by income and location for manufacturing plants, 77–78, 79; distribution of by location for business services facilities, 95; effect of affordable housing programs on, 120; and inner suburban manufacturing facilities, 153; and manufacturing deconcentration, 47–48, 50–51; racial discrimination and, 165 n.19
Special assessment districts, 103

Specialized access to appeal or
    rewards, 119–20
Special service and taxing districts,
    122–24, 129, 131, 132
Spillover costs, 20
Sprawl, 18; defined, 41
Spread effects, of employment
    deconcentration, 31–33, 41–42
Strip malls, 43
Subdivisions, limitations on, 108
Subsidies, calculation of, 144–45
Suburban housing programs,
    100, 116–17, 131; effect
    on costs and benefits of
    employment deconcentration,
    120; financing, 118–19;
    inclusionary zoning, 119;
    other approval-process-based
    mechanisms, 119–20; planning
    programs, 117
Suburban Job Link, Chicago, 114
Suburbs: American attitudes
    toward, 11; likelihood of
    housing abandonment, 45;
    poverty in, 163 n.2; resistance
    to job development, 35. See also
    Inner suburbs
Supplementary workers, 30; in
    business services, 91; and
    vehicle ownership, 164 n.12;
    wage differences in city and
    suburbs, 69–70

Tax-base sharing, 101, 121–22, 131
Taxes: advantage to homeowners,
    61–62, 93, 99, 144, 154, 157;
    breaks to new businesses, 71;
    flight from, 52; savings to inner
    suburban business services
    facilities, 157
Time, value of, 38, 65
Tindale, Steven A., 105
Toronto, 109
Traffic accidents, 34; calculation
    of, 138–39; cost of, 164 n.13;
    distribution of costs across
    income and location, 75–76; in

inner suburbs, 153; social costs
    of, 39–40
Traffic congestion, 24, 32;
    and business services
    deconcentration, 92;
    calculation of, 138–41;
    calculation of distribution,
    149–50; distribution of
    costs across income levels,
    74–75; in inner suburbs,
    153; and manufacturing
    deconcentration, 34, 35–39;
    theory of costs, 37–39
Traffic congestion pricing, 101–3,
    130, 131
Transfer payments, 31
Transportation Efficiency Act for
    the 21st Century, 113, 114
Treyz, George, 32
Tri-State Expressway, 38
Trondheim, 102
Truck transportation, 23
Twin Cities Metropolitan Council,
    128

Unigov system, Indianapolis–
    Marion County, 127
Un/Underemployment. See Spatial
    mismatch of jobs
Urban Development Action Grants,
    124
Urban economic theory, 53;
    location theory, 163 n.4;
    location theory, monocentric
    model, 159
Urban growth boundaries, 109
Urban Institute, 40
Urban medical centers, 16
User charges, 103

Wage differential: city versus
    inner suburbs, manufacturing
    workers, 154–55; city versus
    outer suburbs, business services
    workers, 93–94; city versus
    outer suburbs, manufacturing
    workers, 67–70; city versus

suburbs, 69–70, 159; city versus
suburbs, calculation of, 147–48
Wage gradient, 67, 159
Washington, D.C., population
increase versus land area
increase, 13
Washington, Harold, 122
Welfare levels, 160–61
Welfare-to-work programs, 115
White, Michelle, 67

Wilson, William Julius, 125
Winston, Clifford, 38
Wolman, Harold, 125
Women: commuter travel time, 36;
high value of commuting time,
67–68; lower wage levels, 64,
93–94; proportion of among
business services workers, 90

Zoning, 108, 116; exclusionary, 121;
inclusionary, 119